The 10 Best Ways to Invest In Commercial Real Estate

By

George Donohue

The Ten Best Ways to Invest In
Commercial Real Estate
Copyright © 2020 by George F. Donohue
All Rights Reserved.

Graphic Design by Jenny Bijleveld
Edited by T. Alexis Waleski

George F. Donohue
Visit my website at www.george-donohue.com

Printed in the United States of America

First Printing: March 2020
Lightning Press

ISBN- 978-1-7334026-4-4

2

Table of Contents

Chapter 1: Introduction – Benefits of Diversification

Diversification is the single most important and useful idea in investing. Different investment choices work better under different conditions and in an unreliable world where the future is mostly unknown, a diversified portfolio is a sensible choice.

Every time you visit a doctor, you'll be told, "You need to have a balanced lifestyle: work, home, exercise, diet, and rest." One of the things most doctors will emphasize is a diversified diet.

From when you were a little child you were told you cannot only eat chicken nuggets. You were introduced to many foods and encouraged to try many kinds of meals. When you got to health classes, they explained that your body needs diversity to work properly. The same goes for your investments. You needs to have different kinds of investments—and within each type of investment you need variety.

Yes, you were taught to eat proteins, grain, dairy, and vegetables—but is it healthy to eat the same chicken, potatoes, milk and broccoli for *every* meal? You'll find there are many types of proteins, starches, dairy and vegetables.

This book will explain to you the ten best ways to diversify your real estate investments. These categories are equivalent to your food groups and so you can see you have a lot of choices even in each category to create investments that work well for you. Or if you don't diversify there is huge potential for failure. History has shown what can happen if you only choose one- if you only have potatoes every day....

On a typical day in 1844, the average adult Irishman ate about 13 pounds of potatoes. At five potatoes to the pound, that's 65 potatoes a day. The average for all men, women, and children was a more modest nine pounds, or 45 potatoes. If you want to understand the devastation wrought by the notorious fungus *Phythophthora infestans*, you must begin with those astonishing numbers.

The fungus arrived mysteriously in the fall of 1845. Within a year, potato output had fallen by half, and the newspapers were filled with accounts of gruesome starvation. In another year, output fell by another 80 percent and starvation was no longer newsworthy. By the end of the decade, roughly a million—maybe 12 percent of the population—had perished.

If there's an economic lesson to be learned from the Great Famine, it's that it pays to diversify. Near-total reliance on a single crop invites near-total disaster. The likelihood of that disaster might be small but its potential magnitude makes it worth planning for. (Landsburg, 2001)

Three key advantages of diversification include:
1. *Minimizing risk of loss.* If one investment performs poorly over a certain period, other investments may perform better over that same period, reducing the potential losses of your investment portfolio from concentrating all your capital under one type of investment.
2. *Preserving capital.* Not all investors are in the accumulation phase of life. Some who are close to retirement have goals oriented towards preservation of capital, and diversification can help protect your savings.
3. Generating returns, Sometimes investments don't perform as expected, by diversifying you're not merely relying upon one source for income.

Commercial real estate is an important piece of an investment portfolio. Investors who first think about investing in commercial real estate properties often think about the more straightforward approach of buying a two- or three-family house.

This book explores the various ways one can invest in commercial real estate. It covers in depth the traditional methods as well as opportunities of which you may not have been aware.

Before investing in commercial real estate, investors should self-reflect to determine what is the right way for them to invest.

An investor requires a particular level of key aspects or attributes for each of the commercial investment types cited in the book. These include:
- ready capital to invest
- time you can devote to managing the properties
- inherent or learned talent to own and manage the properties
- the physical ability to carry out your responsibilities
- the time you have to wait to reap the benefits
- proximity to the property

A chart at the end of this book will help you to review your circumstances.

Whether or not you have the items cited above will largely determine what type of commercial investments you should pursue.

Capital

You need money to make an investment. Some authors and supposed investment sages have stated that you can buy real estate with no money down. With very few exceptions, the only people who make money on the idea of purchasing real estate with no money are those who write books about purchasing real estate with no money.

Consider the financial debacles that have happened in the past. The U.S. housing bubble affected over half of the country. Housing prices peaked in early 2006, started to decline in 2006 and 2007, and reached new lows in 2012. The credit crisis resulting from the bursting of the housing bubble was an important cause of the 2007–2009 nationwide recession. Since then, banks have become more conservative in regard to lending money to investors.

Generally speaking, typical lenders will seek approximately 30 percent down to purchase an investment property. From a negotiating point of view, it is better to put more money down or perhaps all cash. If you do, you may be able to strike a better price with the seller since the likelihood that your mortgage will be denied is slim. Thus, you can move more quickly than those who have to get a commercial mortgage approved.

In other words, a seller may give you a better price if you put down 50 percent or more because you are a "sure bet." Another buyer may offer a higher price with only 10 percent down. However, that prospective buyer might find it hard to get a mortgage.

Time

Some real estate investments will require very little of your time. Some investments are very labor-intensive.

Your lifestyle, and how much extra time you may have, will also determine what type of commercial real estate investment is suitable for you.

For example, if you work a nine-to-five job and do not have a lot of free time, you may find it hard to invest in real estate that requires your daily attention.

Talent

Think about the talent and skills that you possess. Your inherent or learned skills may make some investments easier and more lucrative for you. Examine what you do best. Think seriously about what other people say you are good at doing.

Some investments may require a skill you may not have and may take a while to learn. If you lack the needed ability or are not interested in learning the skill, you may need to hire someone else to perform the function for you. This expense could eat into your profit margin. For example a property manager may charge you between three and 10 percent of your gross income.

Physical Ability

Certain commercial real estate investments will require more physical abilities. For example, trying to flip a commercial real estate investment may require a great deal of running around choosing and obtaining materials, making renovations and repairs, selecting and overseeing contractors, or doing the hard work yourself.

In some cases, you will need to have high energy and stamina to get the job done and protect your investment.

The Time to Reap the Benefits

Your patience is another key factor to determine what type of commercial real estate investment you should delve into.

Quite often I ask investor clients, "Are you the stock-playing type or the bond-buying type?" The "stock-players" are more about trading properties like stock brokers trading blue chip stocks, or art collectors buying and selling art work and moving upward in the value of their art collection—or kids who trade baseball cards.

They all do not hold onto the items very long. They try to buy low and sell high.

The bond-buying types want little difficulty, are less risk-oriented and usually want to hold their real estate for a long time. They are generally more apt to accept a lower rate of return than the "stock-trader" types.

Proximity to the Property

Where you are in relation to the investment locale is another consideration.

I usually advise commercial real estate investment beginners "Don't buy anything you can't walk to!"

I don't mean this literally, but you should invest in areas you know, that are in proximity to your home or office. Especially if you are investing in a fixer-upper and you get that call late at night that the heat or electricity went off. You want to be able to get there easily and quickly to resolve it.

As you examine the following opportunities, keep those considerations at the front of your mind.

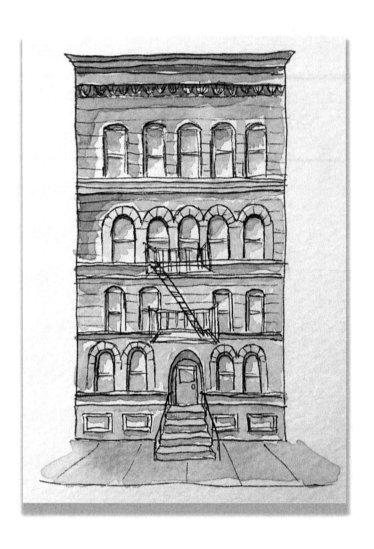

Chapter 2: Small Multi-Family Apartment Property

This chapter deals with the most common way most investors, especially beginners, invest in commercial real estate.

According to the National Multifamily Housing Council's 2017 Tabulation, there are approximately 21,000,000 apartment building in the United States. According to the U.S. Census Bureau, in 2018, there were approximately 119,000,000 households in the U.S.

If you are new to real estate investment, I recommend that you consider buying a small multifamily apartment building. It is the best first stepping-stone to prepare yourself to invest in the other of types of commercial real estate outlined in this book. Buying a small brownstone, row house, or simple apartment building will give you the best basic instructions on the intricacies of owning commercial real estate.

Some people contemplate starting off in commercial real estate by buying a one- or two-family house. I think this choice has more negatives than positives. I strongly recommend the purchase of a three-family house.

Why?

If you buy a one family house, for example, a typical suburban home, you will only have one tenant. If that one tenant becomes problematic, refuses to pay rent, or is always late paying rent, it could cause you some financial as well as mental stress.

A two-family house will reduce your risk somewhat because the odds of both tenants not paying rent at the same time are low. If you need to live in the investment property you are buying then you really are only getting income from one unit and then you are in the same predicament as mentioned in the paragraph above.

I advise you to begin your commercial real estate investment by buying a three-family home. In this way, you can live in the property and have two streams of income from the two tenants. If one tenant becomes problematic you will still have the other income stream. When you make an improvement to the property—for example, changing out the hot water heater—you are also improving your living space.

The physical work to maintain a two-family home is the same as a three-family home. In addition, if you live in the building it is very easy to "commute" to the property to collect the rent and monitor the tenants.

What You Need to Review: Due Diligence

Before you purchase a small apartment building, key items need to be obtained, and key points of information must be reviewed. This is called *due diligence*.

Due diligence is a legal phrase that describes the act of making an appropriate level of investigation when considering a decision: being appropriately cautious. *Due diligence* often refers to the process of vetting a business that is for sale, looking at its assets and liabilities. *Due diligence* is also used to mean taking the necessary precautions to avoid the commission of an offense. The phrase *due diligence* is a combination of the words *due,* derived from the Latin word *debere* which means to owe, and *diligence,* derived from the Latin word *diligentia,* which means carefulness or attentiveness. The term *due diligence* has been in use in a legal sense since the mid-1400s.

Things You Need to Look Into

The most important initial step in purchasing a commercial real estate property is to gather all the relevant information related to the property.

When people make bad investments, it is often because they were too eager to own a property and so did not collect all the relevant information. They made their decision on partial, incomplete data. The missing items, that had information they never saw, were the reasons for their financial disaster. Other investors were given inaccurate, misleading information which led them to make investment blunders.

Some investors I have met were not experienced enough to know what to ask for so they assumed they had everything they needed. Their lack of knowledge cost them greatly.

The following is a list of items you need to have provided for you—and which you must personally examine. If you are not sure how to read or interpret the information, you need to have a trusted adviser explain the good, the bad and the ugly of it.

When you tell sellers and brokers that you need the following items, some will complain that the list is too long—or they will proclaim (perhaps falsely), "No one ever asked for all this information."

Ignore them. It is in your best interest to get the information. "Trust but Verify."

Here is a basic list of items you should become familiar with. Ideally, you should memorize the list.

1.   Copy of the Deed

It is extremely important to get a copy of the deed. You will need to make sure that there are no liens, covenants or encumbrances related to the property. For example, a restriction could prevent you from making certain type of improvements on the property. Or there could be an easement, by which people are allowed to cross your property. An easement and/or a restrictive covenant are red flags. They could be the reason why a property's price seems unusually low.

2.   As-Built Floor Plans

When a building is designed the drawings are initially called construction plans or design plans. Once the building is built the drawings are modified to reflect exactly how the building was built—hence the term "as-built."

3.   Title Abstract Information

The word *title* means the ownership status of the property. It is important to know that the title does not have any problems. There are different grades of titles. A title that is under some type of legal cloud should raise another red flag.

4.   Copy of Any Existing Mortgages

Copies of any and all existing mortgages can raise concerns or open doors. Perhaps the mortgage can be assumable. If the interest rate on the existing mortgage is lower than the rate you can get it may be better to try and assume the seller's mortgage.

5.   Building Department Information About Pending Violations

Every Building Department in every town maintains records of violations. Existing violations need to be cured, and this can be costly. More importantly, if you buy a building and you did not know there was an existing violation in regard to safety—and then someone gets hurt or dies because of this violation, you could be liable for heavy damages.

6.   Zoning Map from the Municipality Showing the Property

You must be able to use the building for the purpose that it was marketed as providing. Sometimes sellers will misrepresent what can actually be built on the site. Make sure that the zoning matches the use. Also, you should determine whether the building's zoning can easily be changed or modified.

7.   Site Plan

A site plan will show how the building sits on the land. This is important because it will delineate how far the building is from the front property line, the back property line and the side lines. Each town has a rule on how far you can be from these property lines. They are called *setbacks*. The site plan should also show where the approved deck or garage sits on the property.

8.   Utility Bills in Summer and Winter

Be sure you have a good understanding of these bills. Sometimes the seller will only show you the months they did not use a lot of electricity or fuel. Insist on seeing bills for the whole year.

9.   Copies of All Leases

Reading the leases thoroughly will give you a good idea about the future of the property. Some tenants may be moving out soon. Or the leases may all be expiring on the same date. If all tenants leave at once that could put you in a very bad situation.

10.   Insurance Policy

Reviewing the insurance policy will give you a good idea of the typical insurance specifications and cost. The existing insurance company might be good for you to use since the existing owner may already have shopped around for the best price.

11.   Water and Sewer Bills

Reviewing the sewer bills and other utility bills will alert you if there are any outstanding balances. Normally, the utility will not seek payment from you for the existing property owner's bills. However, the utility could make your life difficult—if, for instance, they do not want to transfer the utility.

12.   Appraisal

It is sometimes difficult to get the appraisal that was done by the existing property owner's appraiser or by the bank that was used by the existing property owner. Reviewing this document may alert you to some inconsistencies regarding the present condition of the building. The timing of that prior appraisal will be a factor of whether the stated value has any importance to the present market value of the property.

13.   Warranties/Guarantees

When a roof, boiler, or other expensive part of the house is replaced, or has undergone a major repair, the contractor may issue the property owner a warranty or guarantee. This should be transferred to you.

14.   Rent Roll

Every property owner will use some methodology to track their rent that is paid or owed by his or her tenants. This is called the Rent Roll. Of course, the property owner can fudge these numbers but it is important to see the rents that the property owner claims have been generated. You should then compare those numbers to the Estoppel Certificates (see definition below). This will give you an idea of the reliability of the property. If the Rent Roll does not match the Estoppel Certificates, beware.

15.   Tenant Estoppel Certificates

These are some of the most important documents you need to review. The reason for their importance is that without them, you really don't know how much rent is being generated from the property. Sellers will give you rent rolls or perhaps copies of the leases but how do you really know what rent is being collected? A Tenant Estoppel Certificate is basically a letter that each tenant signs and notarizes that cites exactly how much the tenant is paying, how much they paid for their security deposit, when the lease ends, and whether they are behind in their rent.

16.   Financial Statements

Owners of properties should have some kind of financial statements that explain the income and expenses of the properties. Some are very detailed in their accounting and some are not as meticulous. These are not confidential documents. They should be made available to you. If the seller refuses to give them to you, buy at your own risk.

17.   Tax Documents: Schedule E of the 1040 Personal Income Tax Return, the K-1 of a 1065 from a Partnership Return, and an 8825 from 1120S for a S Corporation Return

Schedule E is part of Form 1040 of an Income Tax Return. It is used to report income and losses from rental property on a personal tax return. Income from trusts, estates, partnerships and S corporations are reported on a K-1 and 8825 and subsequently on the Schedule E of the individual partners and shareholders in the case of the partnership and corporation. An honest seller should be able to provide you with a copy of the Schedule E. It will show you if the property is making or losing money.

18.   Leases Related to any Equipment in the Property

Get a list of the equipment that may be included in the purchase. Some equipment may not be owned by the property owner. It may be leased. I recall an investor buying a restaurant thinking the price included the equipment. The week after the sale the owners of the cash registers, jukebox, sound system, large food scales, large-screen TVs, cappuccino machine, etc. came and took all the equipment. It was all leased, so the new owner was not entitled to it.

19.   Certificate of Occupancy

A Certificate of Occupancy is issued by the local Building Department. The C of O will tell you what uses can and cannot be permitted on the property. You need to match this up with what the seller or the seller's representative claims is be permitted.

20.   Real Estate Tax Bills and Assessments for the Past Three Years

Buyers often take the word of the seller with regard to the annual taxes that need to be paid. You should ask for the last three years of real estate tax statements, and examine the trends, if any. If, each year the taxes have gone up by three percent, it's more than likely that they will continue to increase at a rate of about three percent. Consider whether the cumulative effect of this expense could become a hardship.

21. Licenses Related to the Building (e.g., Liquor License)

When you purchase a property there may be a license attached to the building. Get a copy so that you (or your lawyer) can research to see if there are any bad marks against this license. It could possibly affect the value of the building.

22. Landmarks Designation

The property you are about to buy may be landmarked. If it is landmarked it could become a burden to you, because you might not be allowed to do certain things with the building—or you might be compelled to do certain things with the building.

23. Security Deposit Bank Account Statement

If your property has tenants, they probably paid the present owner a security deposit. These tenants will become yours, and when they leave, they will seek to have their deposits returned. Those deposits must be transferred over to you so that you can return all or part of them when they leave. The seller is supposed to keep these funds in a separate bank account and is not supposed to co-mingle them with their own bank account.

24.   Property Management Contract

Some sellers may have hired a property management company to manage and maintain the property. Often, they are paid a percentage of the collected rents. Sometimes these contracts cannot be broken if a new owner takes over the property, and you may be stuck for the length of that contract with property managers you do not want.

25.   Phase I Environmental / Historical Site Assessment

This is a report or study that is prepared for a particular real estate property to determine if the property has exiting or potential environmental contamination liabilities or historic resources. It is a basic step and the first step if more detailed assessment is needed. Phase 1 may include a visit to the property to see if there are any hazardous materials present such as asbestos, lead paint, a chemical spill in underground tanks, mold, etc. It may also include interviewing people related to the property (old owner, new owner, tenants, etc.). It also includes reviewing public files and historical records and maps about the property.

26.   Phase II Environmental / Historical Site Assessment

A Phase II Environmental Site Assessment is a much more in-depth analysis of the property. If a Phase II exists on the property this may be a cause for alarm because someone may have suspected the site had some significant environmental problems in the past. The Phase II tests items such as the soil, ground water, building materials, resources, etc. Usually it is done because the suspected presence of contamination and the study is trying to determine the extent of it and the possible remediation. A Historical Phase II or III may have mitigated any previously unknown history of the site or may have resulted in agreements with state historical offices to redesign the impacts on the property. These agreements may prevent potential modifications/expansions to the property plan.

You need to know whether the remediation was carried out and whether it was done correctly and completely. If it was not, this could be a very costly situation for you.

27.   LEED Certification

LEED is an acronym for Leadership in Energy and Environmental Design. It is a certification program based on a point system. The higher the building scores the better the building is in regard to its energy efficiency and its design related to its impact on the environment. Having a good "green" building is advantageous in that it makes the building more marketable—and often the building uses less energy to carry out its functions which in turn should save you money. LEED has four levels of certification: Certified (40 to 49 points); Silver (50 to 59 points); Gold (60 to 79 points); and Platinum (80 or more points).

28.   Contaminants Audit/Statement

Some older buildings may contain asbestos, lead paint, or radon. It is important that you get the seller or to make a legal representation that clearly states if each of these materials are present in the building, or that they are not. Asbestos and radon are dangerous to inhale; lead paint can inflict serious health consequences if taken internally, especially to children. If your building is contaminated with any of these materials, and your tenant gets sick on account of them, you will be liable.

29.   List of Included Personal Property

As you must have a list of all items that may be leased to a third party, you need to determine all items that will be included in the purchase of the property. Sometimes buyers assume that what they see in the property will remain there. For example, you may assume that items like the washing machines, dryers, chandeliers, alarm systems, whirlpool baths, sound systems, etc. are coming along with the property—only to find, when you move in, that they have disappeared.

30.   List of Trade Fixtures

In some transactions there may be trade fixtures inside the property. Trade fixtures are items such as display counters, signs, HVAC equipment, certain machines, etc. Similar to personal items a buyer needs to be sure if the trade fixtures are being purchased along with the property or if they will be removed by the seller.

57 MONTGOMERY PL

9/10 ©

Chapter 3: Rezoning Play

Successful, profitable rezoning plays that have been carried out by investors who could see well beyond the existing structure. An investor who wants to create and complete a rezoning project must be a visionary.

Here is a good example of a successful rezoning that satisfied all parties involved.

I was asked by one of the leaders of the Methodist Church to sell one of their churches that was located in a beautiful part of upstate New York. The Methodist Church congregation was changing and the Church was smartly and strategically buying and selling assets to accommodate the shift in their church-goers.

This particular Church was built in 1823.

The church was very beautiful but the base building systems such as the electricity and heating system were in need of repair. The church also had a very antiquated bathroom facility. It was extremely challenging to market the property.

Another important consideration when managing a rezoning play is if the building is iconic or an important fixture in a community – something that is beloved by the local residents – you may have a great deal of resistance to changing it or knocking down all or part of it. The way that the ULURP and SEQRA processes work today, it could be a very frustrating, expensive ordeal.

ULURP (Uniform Land Use Review Procedure) is a standardized procedure whereby applications affecting the land use of the city would be publicly reviewed. In 1975, the state of New York passed the State Environmental Quality Review Act (SEQRA) to better establish a process when looking to add new developments on a site. This applies to any group that is deciding to approve a funded sponsored action through private or public financials. These groups include the following;

- Authorities
- Special Boards
- Districts
- Local Government
- State Government

Any project or action classified under Type I has to follow SEQRA requirements. A Type I action is any class of actions that will inevitably have significant impacts on the environment.

You will need to follow an 11-step process when satisfying the SEQRA requirements.

Step 1: Is the action being taken subject to SEQRA? If yes, then it needs to be classified as a type II Action or Type I Action.

Step 2: The correct environmental assessment form needs to be completed and reviewed.

Step 3: A coordinated review is set up by all agencies involved in Type 1 Actions.

Step 4: This is the step where the agency that is taking the lead will make its determination on the significance.

Step 5: The preparation of the draft Environmental Impact Statement (EIS) is started by the lead agency or the applicant.

Step 6: The lead agency that received the draft EIS has 45 days to review and see if it is the draft is adequate for public review.

Step 7: The publishing notice that the EIS has been accepted for the public review.

Step 8: After the notice of completion of the EIS a public comment period then begins.

Step 9: A debate on whether a public hearing should be held.

Step 10: This is where the lead agency is held accountable for checking the precision on the final EIS statement. This should be finalized 45 days after the final hearings or 60 days after the filing of the draft EIS.

Step 11: The final step is involves each agency writing their own SEQRA findings statement for that project. This has to be completed after the final EIS statement and before the final decision the agency makes. Findings certify that the project has met requirements of Part 617. (State Environmental Quality Review Act, 2019)

Keeping this in mind, my strategy was to find a buyer that would not only keep the church standing but actually restore it to its glory.

I knew that another type of Church would not want to buy it because (A) the cost to renovate it would be prohibitive for another church, (B) the demographics and demand for another church in that area did not support the idea of selling it to another church. However, to be certain, we did contact other church denominations and concluded there was no interest in another church buying the property.

I then embarked on the strategy that instinctively I knew would work.

The question really was, who would want to buy this building from 1823 and had the following personal characteristics:

- Someone who would keep the building standing;
- Would improve it without damaging its integrity;
- Had the funds to do a rezoning;
- Could rezone it easily;
- Would select a rezoning the local citizens would appreciate;
- Had the ability to fix all the antiquated systems?

The answer was: an architect seeking a summer country home.

I had maintained over the years a database of the top 600 architects in America. I sent an email to all 600 and explained the situation—and asked them if they were seeking a project that could maintain the beauty of this American architectural gem.

Of the 600 top architects, a handful replied with great interest. Of these, one architect in particular who had an office in Manhattan was seeking to do a personal design/build project for a vacation home and this church proved to be the ideal project for him. He bought the church and because he had good architectural knowledge and a great love for American architecture, he was able to rezone the building to a private residence and bring the building back to its glorious splendor. The successful rezoning made many people happy and satisfied.

I was able to complete my assignment I promised the Methodist Church: to find a creditworthy, motivated buyer. The Church was able to sell the property to someone who would maintain its beauty and fix it up so it would be standing in the community for another 150 years. The community was pleased that the church would be improved and remain a beautiful icon in the area and that a new respectful resident would maintain it. The architect obtained an exceptional, spacious country home.

This story also contains the element of history. This can be another hurdle in a successful rezoning.

In 1966 Congress passed the National Historic Preservation Act (NHPA) and many states followed suit. A significant historical structure or location can come under the prevue of National Historic Preservation Act (NHPA), State Historic Preservation Act (SHPA) or Landmarks Commission. Listing of a property or area on the National and State Registers by itself does not limit the private uses of the property. Owners of property eligible to be listed are sometimes opposed to listing, because they think it automatically regulates what they may do with their property.

In fact, private owners of properties on the National and State Registers may alter or demolish their properties without any regulatory restraints, provided they have not accepted federal funds for repair or renovation of the property or there is no limiting local law. There are three benefits to property owners from being listed on the registers:

1. protection from the effects of federal and state agency actions through a notice, review and consultation process;
2. eligibility for 20 percent federal income tax credits for the costs of substantial rehabilitation; and
3. priority consideration when federal and state agencies are seeking rental space. (SERIES, 2011)

A review should be completed to see if buildings, structures, districts, objects and sites significant to the history, architecture, archaeology and culture are on the National Register of Historic Places, SHPO or Landmarks Commission are in the vicinity of the property you are looking at to rezone. This could affect the outcome of the final plans.

Environmental Issues Related to Rezonings

Some of the most challenging (and sometimes deal-killing) aspects to a potential rezoning are possible environmental issues. When a building is initially designed for a particular use—let's say, light manufacturing or product assembly—the space may have been allowed to use chemicals and materials that are not so environmentally friendly. Or perhaps the use of some materials was acceptable many years ago, when the building was first designed and built. Many environmental issues could be uncovered. It is critically important that you know what you are getting into if you think there could be an environmental challenge.

Here is a list of environmental issues that you may need to address in a rezoning. You can use this as a basic checklist when you inspect your possible building purchase:

ENVIRONMENTAL ASPECTS/POTENTIAL SOURCES OF IMPACT: Check the appropriate box for any environmental hazard or impact associated with the project.

ENVIRONMENTAL ASPECT/IMPACT	Yes √
1. Air emissions: Could the project generate emissions from combustion, dust, greenhouse gases, ozone-depleting substances, or chemical gases?	
2. Chemical Use, Storage, and Inventory: Will the project require the use of lab chemicals, fuel, oils, coolants, cleaners, or solvents?	
3. Soil and Groundwater Contamination: Could project activities impact soil and/or groundwater in any way?	
4. Discharge to Wastewater Systems: Could the project discharge any material to the sanitary sewer?	

5. Surface and Storm water Contamination: Could material from the project contaminate storm water or be discharged to the storm drain system?	
6. Radioactive Materials Reduction and Radioactive Mixed-Waste Generation, Management, Storage, Transportation and Disposal: Will any radiological waste be generated by the project?	
7. Environmental Radiation and Radioactivity: Could any project activities generate and/or release radioactivity?	
8a. Use, Reuse, and Recycling: Are any project activities designed to minimize generation of waste through reuse, recycling, and environmentally preferable purchasing, such as purchasing recycled-content materials?	
8b. Conservation of Resources: Are any project activities designed or expected/intended to conserve natural resources such as water, energy, fuel, etc.?	
9. Construction, Renovation, and Demolition By-Products: Will any project activities generate construction debris or soil stockpiles by clearing or excavation, or disturb lead- or asbestos-containing materials?	

10. Industrial and Hazardous Waste Generation, Management, Storage, Transport and Disposal: Will any unused or spent chemicals, fuel, oils, solvents, PCBs, lead, asbestos, or other hazmat require handling as waste?	
11. Biohazards: Will the project use or generate biological materials, such as microorganisms?	
12. Nanotechnology: Will the project use or generate any nanosubstances?	
13. Archeological Resource Disturbance: Could any project activities impact archeological areas?	
14. Interaction with Wildlife/Habitat: Will the project disturb soil in undeveloped areas or disrupt beehives, bird nests, or other wildlife areas?	
15. Noise: Could the project generate noise that would impact personnel or natural structures?	
16. Water/Sludge for discharge/disposal: Will the project involve boring or drilling that would generate >300 gallons of water/sludge that will require disposal or discharge?	
17. Other?	

Another legal issue that is not related to environmental problems but is part of the Federal law is ADA: the Americans with Disabilities Act.

The ADA is a federal civil rights law that prohibits disability discrimination in various settings—including housing, employment, education, and public accommodations. It prohibits the exclusion of people with disabilities from everyday activities, such as buying an item at the store, watching a movie in a theater, enjoying a meal at a local restaurant, exercising at the local gym, or having a car serviced at a garage. To meet the goals of the ADA, the law established requirements for private businesses of all sizes. These requirements first went into effect on January 26, 1992.

In recognition that many small businesses cannot afford to make significant physical changes to their stores or places of business to provide accessibility to wheelchair users and other people with disabilities, the ADA has requirements for existing facilities built before 1993 that are less strict than for ones built after early 1993 or modified after early 1992. (ADA Access to Buildings and Businesses (Public Accommodations) - Overview, 2019)

Because of its status as law, compliance is not optional. Municipalities do not have to adopt ADA in the way they adopt other building codes, as it is already mandatory. The most recent version of the design standards for public spaces was released by the

Justice Department in 2010 and it is what designers follow today. Keep in mind that similar to codes, things like clear floor space and wheelchair maneuvering space are given in the guidelines as a minimum—you can always design more generously and it's always good practice to keep universal design in mind on any public project.

Public accommodations must remove barriers in existing buildings where it is "readily achievable." This means that removing the barriers is easily accomplishable and able to be carried out without much difficulty or expense, given the public accommodation's resources. To comply with the ADA, a business must take alternative steps to ensure that disabled persons can still reap the benefits of the business or building if barrier removal is not readily achievable. If a business is not open to the public but is only a place of employment like a warehouse, manufacturing facility or office building, then there is no requirement to remove barriers. Such a facility is called a commercial facility.

The ADA requires that newly constructed facilities, first occupied on or after January 26, 1993, meet or exceed the minimum requirements of the ADA Standards for Accessible Design. Alterations to facilities, spaces or elements (including renovations) on or after January 26, 1992, also must comply with the Standards. (Schires, 2017)

The building you are contemplating may not have any improvements that are required by today's ADA.

It is important that you get an ADA expert—most likely a local architect—who can help you make a list of the items that need to improve and the projected cost for each improvement.

ADA requirements are divided into four basic categories to review for ADA compliance.

Priority 1: Accessible approach and entrance
Priority 2: Access to goods and services
Priority 3: Access to rest rooms
Priority 4: Any other measures necessary

Many extensive lists are available on the internet to lead you though your ADA compliance inspection and even then you should have a local professional confirm all regulations.

These are two of the most recommended checklists:

https://www.ada.gov/racheck.pdf

https://www.adachecklist.org/doc/fullchecklist/ada-checklist.pdf

Popular Rezoning Plays Across the Nation

Two of the most popular rezoning plays—and I believe they are some of the best adaptive reuses of a large facility—are the rezoning of major train stations and general post offices.

They are classic examples of large structures that in their early life served a good purpose. However, over time technology changes, management strategies change, demographics change—and all these shifts cause these large structures to become obsolete.

Forward-looking government officials will put these structures out to bid in a Request for Proposal (RFP) to see who in the nation can take a once magnificent structure and design something to meet today's communities' needs.

An RFP is a document that solicits proposal, often made through a bidding process, by an agency or company interested in procurement of a commodity, service, or valuable asset, to potential suppliers to submit business proposals. It is submitted early in the procurement cycle, either at the preliminary study, or procurement stage. With the RFP will come the assurance that a rezoning will be granted if the design makes sense.

Some good examples:

Ansonia Clock Company

The Ansonia Clock Company moved from Ansonia, Connecticut, in 1879, to Brooklyn New York where they built a large factory and hired 350 workers.

A new factory, with Samuel Curtiss, Jr. as the architect was designed as a huge square complex, a block square, centered on an open courtyard, encompassing 12th and 13th Streets, between 7th and 8th Avenues in a neighborhood known as Park Slope. It would be "the largest clock factory in the world," according to the *Brooklyn Eagle Newspaper*. The Brooklyn plant was the sole manufacturer of Ansonia clocks, which had many different models and styles. By 1914, they were at their height, with over 440 clock models, and sales in the US, Europe, Australia, China, India, Japan and 18 other countries.

Unfortunately, several factors (competition, some bad business decisions, World War I, the beginnings of the Depression) killed Ansonia's business, and in 1929 the company was sold to a Russian trading firm.

The building was used by many other industrial concerns over the years, including Globe Lighting Products, whose painted sign can still be seen on the building. This type of factory is perfect for residential reuse, due to its size, access to light on both sides, the courtyard itself, sturdiness and beauty. It's been residential since 1982, the complex is now co-ops, with seventy units, and is now called Ansonia Courts.

Sibley, Lindsey and Curr

Sibley, Lindsay and Curr Building is a historic commercial building located in Rochester in Monroe County, New York. It was designed by noted Rochester architect J. Foster Warner and built for Sibley's in 1904. The original wing of the building was constructed in 1906 as a five-story, Chicago school style skeletal steel building sheathed in brown Roman brick with deeply set Chicago style windows, topped by a clock tower with Baroque and Renaissance style details. Additions were made to the building in 1911 and 1924, including a 12-story tower section.

By 1939, Sibley's was the largest department store between New York City and Chicago. Sibley's was acquired by The May Department Stores Company and the Sibley Building location closed in the early 1990s.

The Sibley Building was formerly home to State University of New York's Monroe County College Downtown Campus, Damon City Campus, which opened in 1991 as the college's second campus and remained in the building until completion of its new Downtown Campus, located in the Kodak Tower, headquarters of the Kodak Company.

It is currently undergoing re-development into a multi-use building. The building is now known as Sibley Square and houses businesses such as High Tech Rochester along with 104 luxury, market-rate apartments branded under *Spectra at Sibley Square*, 21 units for middle-income households, and 72 senior apartments for people 55 and older branded under *The Landmark at Sibley Square*. Retail is also planned for the ground floor of the building. (Sibley's, Lindsay and Curr Building, 2019)

James A. Farley Building

The James A. Farley Building was the main post office for Manhattan and has the iconic saying "Neither snow nor rain nor heat nor gloom of night stays these couriers from the swift completion of their appointed rounds" on the building. The Farley Post Office once held the distinction of being the only Post Office in New York City open to the public 24 hours a day, seven days a week but that ended in 2009. The building was built in 1912 and opened in 1914. The building's size was doubled in 1934 by then Postmaster General James A. Farley, who expanded the general Post Office to The Ninth Avenue side. Postmaster General Farley's historical association to the landmark is due to this expansion. Portions of the landmark James Farley Post Office are being adaptively reused and converted to house a new concourse for Amtrak. The Amtrak facility within the historic Farley Post Office will be named the Moynihan Train Hall. This is considered an expansion of Pennsylvania Station (Penn Station) in Manhattan.

US Post Office Washington, DC

In 1836, fire destroyed the existing post office and patent office building, and plans were made to construct a new building on the site.

The General Post Office was one of three buildings, along with the U.S. Treasury Building and the Patent Office, commissioned by President Andrew Jackson. For the General Post Office, Robert Mills desired a marble exterior, "according to the ancient practice," and upon its 1842 completion it was the first all-marble-clad exterior in the capital.

Thomas Ustick Walter, the architect who designed the Capitol dome, oversaw the General Post Office's expansion beginning in 1855. Expansion work was halted during the Civil War, and the Union used the building's basement as munitions storage. Sympathetic to the Mills design, Walter's addition was completed in 1866.

After the General Post Office relocated in 1897, over time numerous government agencies occupied the building. In 1919, when the building housed the National Selective Service Board, General of the Armies John J. Pershing ensconced himself there to write his final report on the World War I involvement of the American Expeditionary Force.

The Tariff Commission, later called the U.S. International Trade Commission, was the building's primary 20th-century tenant, occupying it from 1932 to 1988. After some years of vacancy, the building underwent restoration and in 2002 reopened as the Hotel Monaco.

County Chevrolet Car Dealership

Not all rezoning projects have to be mammoth. The former location of County Chevrolet Car Dealer Lot on Main Street in Warwick, N.Y. was approved for rezoning of the one-acre lot. The larger "Central Garage" building now houses three businesses, including a Super Cuts hair salon, a 2,600-square-foot restaurant, and a 1,800 square-foot Dunkin Donuts. What was initially a former car dealership was renovated and now contains three income bearing businesses in a busy downtown.

Rezoning Plays

One of the most exciting, interesting commercial real estate plays is to buy a property intending to rezone the lot and repurpose the property.

The tactic is to find an obsolete building— one that no one wants anymore, that is out of fashion, not useable for its initial design, and is vacant. Such buildings are normally not expensive relative to other properties in a particular market.

Once you have located an undesirable property, you need to put your creativity, vision and imagination to work. You need to ask yourself, "What uses are trendy now or may soon be trendy? Can I transform this broken-down building so that it can take advantage of how the market is going?"

If you can buy something unwanted for a very low price, then add your creative genius and create a much-wanted object that people will pay a premium for, great. But to realize that vision, you sometimes have to persuade the local government to rezone the property: make it permissible for the property to be used in the way that you envision.

For example, if you want to turn a single-family dwelling into an office building, you might come up against a zoning law that designates that neighborhood as strictly residential. In that case, you would need to have the lot on which your building sits, at least, rezoned as commercial.

Or suppose you have a long driveway behind your house, and a big back yard on which you would like to build rental units. You might have to have your driveway rezoned as a street, to make that construction legal.

The challenge to the rezoning plays is that you need to have an architect and/or zoning expert help you make the idea into a reality.

Here are some zoning terms and procedures to give you a better understanding on what a rezoning play can entail.

A

Accessory Use. Land uses within a property that are—in addition to the parcel's principal use—customary, appropriate, subordinate, incidental to, and serve the principal use. The governing body often includes in its zoning ordinance specific accessory uses it believes meet these criteria, but as an example, typical residential accessory uses include garages, decks, swimming pools, and storage sheds.

Aesthetic Regulation. Aesthetic zoning regulations are used to maintain aesthetic features within a district by permitting only uses, designs and structures that conform to or complement the area's existing uses and structures. Examples of aesthetic regulations are limitations on parking, setbacks, the colors and architecture of structures, and types of landscaping, roofs, and building materials.

Amortization. When a building or use becomes non-conforming due to a change in zoning regulations, the property will be given a period of time to comply with the new regulations. This is called the amortization period. If a property is not compliant within the amortization period, the use will be prohibited.

Ancillary Uses. Such uses are permitted land uses that are secondary and complementary to the principal use, but not accessory. An example of an ancillary use is an office supply store in an office park that only serves the principal office uses within the district.

B

Bulk Regulations. These regulations control the size and layout of structures, including regulations as to open space, lot lines, maximum building height, and maximum floor area ratio.

Buffer Zones. When two adjacent districts have in-compatible permitted uses, in order to reduce the conflict between the uses, the governing body may require a buffer zone. Typically such zones will include park areas, grass, trees or berming. Such zones are commonly used when the development of a multi-family complex is proposed adjacent to a single-family district.

C

Commercial Use. These uses, permitted only in commercial districts, typically include wholesale, retail, or service business uses operating for profit, including office uses.

Comprehensive/General Plan. A long-term planning instrument that sets forth policies for the future development of the jurisdiction in a manner that will satisfy the jurisdiction's goals, e.g., maintain orderly growth and protect the general welfare. Comprehensive plans often include local area plans, land use-related resolutions by the governing body, maps, and policy statements.

Conditional Use. These uses are permitted on a permanent basis within a district so long as the governing body's conditions are met. These uses require conditions because without them, they could negatively impact the parcel or bordering properties. Permits for conditional uses are given at the discretion of the governing body.

Contract Zoning. Contract zoning occurs when a property owner and the governing body enter an agreement that the property will be rezoned and the owner will accept the body's use and design restrictions.

Cumulative Zoning. Under this zoning scheme, property zoned for specific uses can be used for that use and for less intensive uses. For example, an area zoned for multi-family uses would also permit a single-family use within the parcel.

D

Density. Density is the amount of development allowed per acre, and typically calculated by the number of dwelling units per acre (for residential) or floor area ratio (for commercial).

Discriminatory/Exclusionary Zoning. This type of zoning refers to a community's use of zoning regulations to exclude certain groups of people. Though it is unlawful to expressly exclude people based on race or ethnicity, regulations relating to development densities can have exclusionary effects. For example, communities will limit the number of dwellings permitted, reducing the housing supply, and thus lowering opportunities for new buyers. Further, reducing the housing supply increases market prices, having the effect of excluding lower-income families. Similarly, zoning regulations that limit or prohibit low-income multi-family complexes have the direct effect of excluding lower-income households from residing in the community.

Down-Zoning. Down-zoning occurs when a parcel is rezoned to a classification permitting only less intensive uses. Communities will employ down-zoning to limit less-desired intensive uses. For example, a community may rezone a parcel from a multi-family designation to a single-family district.

E

Exactions. New development will often increase the use of, and the need for, improved or new public infrastructure and facilities, e.g., water and sewer lines, road improvements, and parks. Exactions are how a community forces developers to contribute to the cost of such infrastructure. They can take the form of requiring a developer to pay for a portion of the infrastructure improvements necessitated by the development, impact fees, or the donation of a portion of the developer's land.

F

Floor area ratio (FAR) is the ratio of a building's total floor area (gross floor area) to the size of the piece of land upon which it is built. The terms can also refer to limits imposed on such a ratio through zoning.

Floating Zones. These are districts that are permitted under the zoning ordinance, but not placed on the zoning map. They are typically employed for uses that are anticipated in the future (e.g., major entertainment centers, intensive industrial uses), but no specific location has been identified within the community. When an application is made for such a use on a specific parcel, a floating zone can be established and located on the zoning map, provided the regulations set forth in the zoning ordinance are met.

G

Grandfather Clause. This term is a poor description for a legal prior non-conforming use. A "grandfathering" situation occurs when an existing use was in compliance with zoning regulations at the time it began, but changes to the regulations have caused the use to become non-conforming. If the owner sells the property, the buyer will have the right to continue the non-conforming use, causing people to label the use as "grandfathered." However, because this situation is simply the transfer of a lawful non-conforming use, the laws related to such uses create certain limitations, e.g., the use may not continue indefinitely as it will be subject to an amortization period, and the use cannot be expanded.

I

Industrial Uses. These are non-residential, non-agricultural, non-commercial uses such as mining, milling, and manufacturing. Zoning ordinances generally include many classes of industrial uses, and the regulation of each varies depending on the intensity and impact of the use. Common examples of light industrial uses are warehouses, manufacturing and distribution where they operate without negative impacts on the surrounding uses. Heavy industrial uses have the potential to create public nuisance conditions (e.g., noise, environmental impacts), and are thus more stringently located and regulated. Examples of heavy industrial uses include quarries, landfills, and asphalt or concrete mixing plants.

M

Master Plan. The overall plan for a community's development. A master plan must be consistent with the goals and policies described in the comprehensive/general plan and other local plans, e.g., an area plan. Generally master plans include the location of proposed land uses, description of the types of uses, intensities of uses, and building and structure limitations, though they may also include descriptions of desired parking, open space, and layout.

Mixed-Use Designation. This designation allows integration of multiple types of uses within a single district—for example, a development that includes multi-family residential, retail and office uses.

Moratorium. When a governing body is considering the amendment of its zoning ordinance or planning documents, it may decide to enact a temporary ban, a "moratorium," on zoning applications for the uses being considered. It is generally accepted that a body has the right to use moratoriums in order to gain time to make sound planning decisions, because landowners seeking to develop their properties will be delayed (or, prevented from developing in the event the ultimate change prohibits the use they intended). However, the moratorium must be reasonable. In determining reasonableness, courts have considered whether the moratorium advances a legitimate governmental interest, is being made in good faith, and doesn't deprive the landowner of all reasonable use for too long.

N

New Urbanism. New urbanism is a planning and design concept based primarily on two objectives: neighborhoods should have a sense of community and be environmentally friendly. To affect these goals, new urbanists lobby and work with communities to create or amend planning and zoning laws to allow neighborhoods with multiple uses, require communities to be designed for pedestrian and car traffic, and require environmentally conscious building designs and construction.

NIMBY. An acronym for Not In My Backyard, NIMBY refers to groups that oppose a new land use near their residential property. NIMBY efforts are directed at every type of use they deem incompatible with their residential use, including commercial retail or offices, industrial, or more intensive housing. The arguments against such uses near residential neighborhoods include that they will increase car and truck traffic, noise and crime, and lower property values. The power of such opposition is largely political, with a group appealing to their elected officials to deny approval of the opposed project.

Non-Conforming Use. Any use, structure or building that doesn't comply with the applicable zoning regulations. Where the use was originally in compliance, but a regulations change made it non-compliant, the use became a lawful prior non-conforming use (LPNCU). As the name suggests, LPNCUs are lawful, and may continue, but they face certain restrictions. Common restrictions are:

1. the use must be made compliant within a certain period of time (an amortization period);
2. the use cannot be expanded;
3. if the LPNCU is changed, it may not return to the prior use;
4. where the property is damaged beyond a certain point, it may not be repaired.

O

Open Space. Spaces for public or private uses for enjoyment, such as park areas or simply green space. Open space requirements are often calculated as a certain percentage of a parcel's size.

P

Planned Unit Development (PUD). A mixed-use development (often residential, retail and office) with a cohesive design plan. To encourage the feasibility of such developments, zoning regulations, otherwise required of the individual uses, may be waived or modified to allow for flexibility in the development's design.

Primary Use. A primary use is the principal or dominant use of the land, such as residing in a home, running business or manufacturing a product.

R

Regulatory Taking. A taking in the real property arena refers to the government exercising its power of eminent domain to acquire ownership of private property for a public use or benefit. A taking is lawful, but the government must pay for the land acquired. A regulatory taking occurs where a governing body enacts regulations that effectively deprive a landowner of all economically reasonable use or value of their property. While the government doesn't actually take title to the property, because the regulations have made the property essentially worthless, it is viewed as a taking, and thus requires compensation to the landowner.

Residential Districts. These districts permit residential uses, and typically vary depending on lot size and the number of families that the dwellings in the district are meant to house (e.g., single-family, two-family, etc.). Residential districts for multi-family apartments typically consider the number of units within a defined space (e.g., up to 50 units per acre).

Rezoning. Rezoning is simply a change in the zoning district applied to a parcel of land, and thus a change to the permitted uses and accompanying regulations within that parcel.

S

Setbacks. Distances between structures and property lines. They vary depending on the zoning district.

Smart Growth. Similar to New Urbanism, smart growth is an urban development and planning concept stressing mixed-used neighborhoods, walkability, and environmentally conscious development and design.

Spot Zoning. Spot zoning is unlawful, and occurs when a single parcel is zoned differently from surrounding uses for the sole benefit of the landowner. While property may lawfully be zoned differently from surrounding uses, the uses are typically permitted because they serve a public benefit or a useful purpose to the surrounding properties. For example, sound planning policies would permit a school to be located in the center of a residential neighborhood. Locating an adult entertainment store in the same neighborhood would not.

Standard State Zoning Enabling Act (SZEA). Federally developed in 1921, SZEA was a standard act on which states could model their own zoning enabling acts. SZEA provided that legislative bodies could divide their jurisdictions into different districts, made a statement of purpose for zoning regulations, and created procedures for establishing such regulations.

V

Variance. A discretionary, limited waiver or modification of a zoning requirement. It is applied in situations where the strict application of the requirement would result in a practical difficulty or unnecessary hardship for the landowner. Typically, the difficulty or hardship must be due to an unusual physical characteristic of the parcel.

Vested Rights. The vested rights doctrine permits a landowner to build pursuant to a prior zoning regulation when there has been a substantial change of position or expenditures by an innocent party in reliance upon the issuance, or probable issuance, of a building permit. However, where no permit had been issued, and the owner has only an anticipation that it could develop their land under the existing zoning, a change in zoning prohibiting their anticipated development doesn't create a vested right. There is no guarantee that zoning classifications or regulations will stay the same.

Z

Zoning Ordinance. Created in compliance with a governing body's comprehensive plan, zoning ordinances are comprised of maps showing the zoning districts and text setting forth the regulation of uses and structures within each type of district.

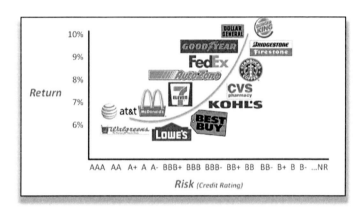

Chapter 4: NNN Tenant Investment

Triple Net Lease investment (usually abbreviated to NNN) is one of the most conservative options for commercial real estate investment. It is a deliberately low-risk play. If you are looking to buy a triple-net-leased property, here are your ordinary requirements:

- The building should be single-story, stand-alone, occupied by a single tenant.

The tenant is usually a well-known retailer. (The most desirable NNN tenants are often chain drugstores, such as Walgreens, CVS, and Rite Aid.)

- The property is easily accessible and on a main road.
- The Tenant takes care of all the expenses.
- The Tenant maintains the entire property, inside and out.
- The lease is long-term (15 years or more).

Typical NNN tenants include:

Necessity Retail:
- CVS
- 7- Eleven
- Walgreens

Fast Food Restaurants:
- McDonalds
- YUM! Brands which include KFC, Taco Bell and Pizza Hut

Dollar Stores/ Discount Retailers:
- Ross, Kohl's and Big Lots
- TJX Companies that includes AJ Wright, T.J. Maxx and Marshalls
Costco
- Walmart and Sam's Club (owned by Walmart
- Family Dollar, Dollar General, Dollar Tree, 99Cents Only

Gas Stations:
- ExxonMobil,
- Chevron,
- ARCO,
- Shell,
- Texaco,
- BP,
- Union 76,
- ConocoPhillips,
- Valero

Business/Communications:

- UPS
- Verizon
- AT&T
- T-Mobile
- FedEx Corporation including FedEx, Kinkos,
- and others

Vehicle Repair/Parts:
- AutoZone,
- Jiffy Lube

Casual and Budget Dining:
- Olive Garden, Red Lobster, and Long Horn Steakhouses are all owned by Darden Restaurants,
- On The Border, Romano's Macaroni Grill, and Chili's are all owned by Brinker International,

Investment-Grade NNN Office -- includes corporate headquarters, distribution facilities, and service locations of large companies with strong credit ratings.
- healthcare
- pharmaceutical
- technology providers,
- business-to-business services,
- consumer goods
- manufacturing facilities, etc.

69

Lease Clauses to Protect You

When you invest in a NNN tenant situation your income and your success hinges on the success of the single tenant. If the tenant does well, you will receive the most attractive upside to any investment: predictable and recurrent income.

However, if the tenant falls upon hard times or the economy affects their sales or their competition outpaces them, you may fall into trouble. If the tenant starts to lag behind in rent and/or can't pay the key operating expenses such as electricity, real estate taxes, insurance, etc. you may be burdened with those bills while not receiving any rental income.

This is where the art of risk management comes in. The great money managers throughout the world do not manage money. They manage risk. To mitigate any negative situations with your NNN tenant you need to be sure that the lease you sign with the tenant has certain clauses that will benefit you and greatly reduce the possibility of financial harm. Be sure to hire a real estate broker/negotiator and a lawyer who are both experts in regard to commercial leasing.

A wonderful highlight of my career came when I was the General Manager of Leasing for the World Trade Center. Each year, I oversaw about 500 different commercial lease transactions. I have seen almost every kind of commercial lease situation, problem, and solution—including those pertaining to NNN leases.

Many clauses must at least be considered for inclusion in a NNN lease. Here are the three I consider the most important:

Right to Audit

The Right to Audit clause basically gives you the ability to ask for the financial statements or at least the sales revenue information of the particular store that occupies your building.

You must remember that if the single tenant that is occupying your building goes bust or has some financial difficulties you may not receive any rent and that could cause you great financial hardship. The Right to Audit is an early warning system. If you have the tenant's sales data sent to you each month, the numbers will give you a heads up if the tenant is heading for financial difficulty that will impact you negatively.

This will give you time to discuss the situation with your tenant and/or give you time to create a Plan B—which might be to renegotiate the lease or find a financially stronger tenant.

Subleasing Rights

It is difficult to insist that a tenant not have the right to sublease or assign the space to another entity. Tenants will try to incorporate escape clauses in the lease: clauses that will allow them to get out of the lease if it becomes onerous or inconvenient to them. If you are going to give a tenant the right to sublease, you need to address three points:

You will want to keep the profits if the tenant subleases to another entity. Quite often, market rents will move upward in great retail locations. If the tenant subleases to another entity following a big increase in the market rent, and the tenant is able to get a great subtenant to pay a higher rent, you should benefit. For example, if your tenant is paying $50 per square foot per year in rent for 10,000 square feet and the market has increased to $80 per square foot per year then you should receive that extra $300,000 per year if the tenant subleases the space to another entity.

Secondly, you want to be very restrictive about what type of entity the tenant can sublease the space to. For example, if your property is triple-net-leased to a top-credit drug chain, they should be able to rent only to another top-credit drug chain. If you let them sublease to anyone, you may have a type of retailer you do not need or one that may hurt neighboring tenants—perhaps in other properties you own. The best strategy is to have the Use Clause be very specific about what type of use can be allowed in the space.

Restoration Clause

Many times, toward the end of a lease, a tenant will stop paying rent and try to use their security deposit to pay the rent. Or even worse, they try to leave the space without paying the last few months' rent.

When I was managing the leasing of the World Trade Center, I encountered this type of tenant much too often. So, I devised a tactic in which all the leases had a restoration clause. A restoration clause generally states that a tenant must restore the space *exactly* the way you originally gave the space to the tenant. If they had a blue carpet and blue walls ten years ago and then replaced the carpet and painted the walls white, and we triggered the clause, we could force them to bring the carpet back and paint the walls the exact same blue color. If you invoke that clause on a bad tenant, they may find that it will cost them a lot more to restore the space than to simply pay the rent. (We also reminded them they had to wait for us to return their security deposit until after we inspected the space.)

74

Chapter 5: Buying A Retail Condo

When we hear the term condominium (condo for short), we think of a buying a residential condo. This is the most popular type of condo in America. Scholars have traced the earliest known use of the condominium form of tenure to a document from first-century Babylon. The word *condominium* originated in Latin.

The first condominium law passed in the USA was in Puerto Rico in 1958. The first condo in the Continental U.S. was built in Salt Lake City in 1960. Many Americans' first concept of condo life came from South Florida. They used it to sell thousands of inexpensive homes to retiring Northerners with cash. Over the last 30-40 years it has exploded in metropolitan areas such as Miami, San Francisco, Seattle, Boston, Chicago, Austin, Los Angeles and New York City.

There are currently almost 27 million community association (homeowner associations, condos, and housing cooperatives) units in the U.S. The number is projected to rise by 50 percent in the next 20 years.

Community Association Growth

Year	Communities	Housing Units	Residents
1970	10,000	.7 million	2.1 million
1980	36,000	3.6	9.6
1990	130,000	11.6	29.6
2000	222,500	17.8	45.2
2002	240,000	19.2	48.0
2004	260,000	20.8	51.8
2006	286,000	23.1	57.0
2008	300,800	24.1	59.5
2010	311,600	24.8	62.0
2011	317,200	25.4	62.7
2012	323,600	25.9	63.4
2013	328,500	26.3	65.7
2014	333,600	26.7	66.7
2015	338,000	26.2	68.0
2016	342,000	26.3	69.0
2017	344,500	26.6	70.0
2018	347,000	26.9	73.5

(COMMUNITY ASSOCIATIONS IN THE UNITED STATES, n.d.)

There are four sources of retail condo demand.

1.   Retailers seeking flagship locations.

2.   Smaller retailers that buy spaces because they're sick of getting kicked out of retail locations due to rising rents and landlords looking for a higher-tier tenant. These tenants can see a huge appreciation of value that they could never find in a rental space.

3.   Multifamily investors looking for properties unhindered by rent regulations, who only want to deal with one tenant.

4.   Foreign investors drawn in not only by the allure of owning real estate in Manhattan, but by the

76

economic advantages of retail assets with tax abatements, shared common charges, low maintenance, highly capitalized foreign tenants and stable yet higher yields.

Sellers are realizing a higher value in retail asset sales, as opposed to individual residential condo sales, while buyers see less management-intensive operations as a huge factor to increase demand.

In this particular type of investment play the strategy is to purchase a retail condo in a great location. This requires foresight. Will this location still be attractive and desirable 10 or 15 years from now? This "educated guesswork" can be arrived at by looking at demographic trends, what retailers have come and gone, and—if the building is a tower—what type of residents are above the retail space.

The Importance of the Retail Mix
When you purchase a retail condo you should select a property where the retail space can be divided. You might not decide to divide it, but you should have that option. Consider two factors consider before leasing the space to a single tenant:

1. Large retail tenants, especially well-known retailers, always demand a lower rent than if you leased the space to smaller, less popular retailers. The large retailers have good marketing budgets to attract consumers; they have experienced staff that can maintain and

operate the space professionally; you may be able to get a good corporate guarantee.

2. Large tenants do go bankrupt. If you have one single large tenant and they vacate the space suddenly because of poor sales or a bankruptcy, you will have no income and will have to scramble to find another big tenant.

Here are just a few large retailers who were household names that went bankrupt. Please note that these companies cover a broad array of all the segments of the retail industry, from clothes to toys to electronics to vitamins.

- Toys R Us
- Mandee's
- Sears
- Mattress Firm
- David's Bridal
- Brookstone
- Rockport
- Nine West
- Claires
- Gymboree
- Payless
- Radio Shack
- Vitamin World
- Perfumania
- The Limited
- Barneys New York

On the other hand, you will find advantages to leasing your retail condo to one retailer. For starters, you will only have to deal with one tenant—which means only collecting rent from one tenant and only keeping one tenant happy.

One Retailer leasing 10,000 square

The alternative is to divide up your retail condo into a few smaller stores and rent them out individually. Here we have divide the 10,000 square feet into five stores of 2,000 square feet each:

Five Retailers leasing 2,000 square feet each.

The benefit of dividing up the space to accommodate five retail stores is that if one of the stores goes bankrupt or defaults on the lease, at least you will have four other tenants paying their rent, so you still have some cash flow. (The likelihood of five stores going bankrupt at the same time is very, very slim: almost zero.)

The downside of creating this comfort level in your plan is that you will need to spend money on designing the division of the space and then building the walls and five separate entrances.

The "retail mix" within the space will drive the success or failure of this division. A retail mix means having a variety of types of businesses in your space. Hypermarkets, specialty stores, department stores, and convenience stores can all be in one area and reduce your risk of losing all your tenants.

LOAN AGREEMENT

This Loan Agreement is made and will effective on _____ day of _____, 20_____

BETWEEN

[Company Name] with little introduction of the company and the law under which this company is existing with its street address along with city, state and zip code

AND

[Company Name] with little introduction of the company and the law under which this company is existing with its street address along with city, state and zip code

1. Promise to Pay: Within _____ months from today, Borrower promises to pay to Lender_____ dollars ($_____) and interest as well as other charges avowed below.

2. Accountability: Although this agreement may be signed below by more than one person, each of the undersigned understands that they are each as individuals responsible and jointly and severally liable for paying back the full amount.

3. Breakdown of Loan: Borrower will pay
   Amount of Loan: $_____
   Other (Describe) $_____
   Amount financed: $_____
   Finance charge: $_____
   Total of payments: $_____
   ANNUAL PERCENTAGE RATE_____%

4. Repayment: Borrower will pay back in the following manner: Borrower will repay the amount of this note in _____ equal continuous monthly installments of $_____ each on the _____ day of each month preliminary on the _____ day of _____, 20____, and ending on _____, 20____

5. Prepayment: Borrower has the right to pay back the whole exceptional amount at any time. If Borrower pays before time, or if this loan is refinanced or replaced by a new note, Lender will refund the unearned finance charge, figured by the Rule of 78-a commonly used formula for figuring rebates on installment loans.

6. Late Charge: Any payment not remunerated within ten (10) days of its due date shall be subject to a belatedly charge of 5% of the payment, not to exceed $_____ for any such late installment.

7. Security: To protect Lender, Borrower gives what is known as a security interest or mortgage in. [Describe:]
   _____
   _____
   _____
   _____

Loan Agreement Template

82

Chapter 6: Financing a Commercial Real Estate Deal

If you are the purchaser of a commercial real estate property you will either manage the asset yourself or hire a property management company to take care of the building. Physically managing a property can be exhausting, especially if the property is old and different components of the building such as the boiler, water heater, septic system, roof, etc. are near the end of their life cycle. If you do not want to physically take care of a property, or if you do not have the time, a good alternative is to become the bank for a purchaser.

Before there were banks, people loaned money to each other. The origins of banking may have been in ancient Babylon and Old Sangvi. Merchants offered a barter system using loans of grain as collateral. Money Lenders in ancient Greece and the Roman Empire started to accepted deposits and changed money. Evidence in China and India shows that also had money lending at about the same time.

More modern banking can be traced to medieval and early Renaissance Italy. One of the most famous Italian banks was the Medici Bank in 1397. In the 17th and 18th centuries more modern banking practices appeared including reserve banks and the issue of banknotes. London Goldsmiths began storing the possessions of merchants in their own vaults. The Goldsmiths charged a fee for the storage and eventually began to lend out money on their behalf, this began modern banking. The notes of promise to pay became bank notes based on the standard of the goldsmiths vaults. The Bank of England was the first to begin issuing permanent bank notes in 1695.

The root word in "mortgage" is the French word "mort": death. Literally, a mortgage is a "death pledge."

A mortgage is used by the purchasers of real property gather them money to purchase real estate. Or to get money against property they already own using a lien.

In order to help pull the country out of the Great Depression, the Federal Housing Administration (FHA) initiated a new type of mortgage aimed at the folks who couldn't get mortgages in 1934. They increased the loanable amount, extended length of payment, established the amortization of loans, which meant that people got to pay an incremental amount of the loan's principal amount with each interest payment, and set quality standards that homes had to meet in order to qualify for the loan.

You can lend someone money and generate a good recurrent and predictable income for yourself. In essence, you become the bank. The upside to becoming a private lender is that you do not have to physically toil to manage the property; you have predictability of the income; the income can be higher than for less risky investments; the income can be received over a long term.

You'll find great differences between investing money and loaning it. When you invest, the law says that you are willingly putting your money into something where you can risk it all. For example, you can buy a stock with the hope of it rising and/or paying you a dividend. But if that company goes bankrupt, your investment can be wiped out.

On the other hand, when you loan money the law says you have the right to be repaid, and legal remedies exist to help you get your money back. Another important benefit to lending money as a bank, is that if the borrower defaults on the loan, you have the right to take over the property.

In a real estate transaction, the borrower might put up 30 percent of the money to buy the building, and you lend the buyer 70 percent of the purchase price. Another way to look at it is that you are in the senior position and the borrower is in the junior position—because you are risking more capital.

The problem is that when the buyer purchases the building the deed is often put into the borrower's name. If the borrower defaults, your challenge will be to sue the borrower to get the deed out of his name and into yours.

Chapter 7: Investing in REIT stocks

One of the easiest ways to invest a portion of your money into commercial real estate is to invest in a Real Estate Investment Trust: a REIT. These trusts are sometimes called "real estate stock." REITs are corporations that own and manage a portfolio of real estate properties and mortgages. Anyone can buy shares in a publicly traded REIT. They offer the benefits of real estate ownership without the headaches or expense of being a landlord. Public REITs are purchased through a stock exchange. Private REITs are not publicly traded.

There are many types of REITS. Here is a small sample of the areas that REITS can focus on:

Type of REITS	When Acquired
General Real Estate REITS	
Shopping Center REISTS	
Resort and Hotel REITS	
Office Building REITS	
Data Center REITS	
Industrial REITS	
Infrastructure REITS	
Timberland REITS	
Mortgage REITS	
Single Family Home REITS	
Student Housing REITS	

Many REIT investors diversify and invest in various types of REITs. Others focus on REITs that specialize in a specific type of real estate.

90

Chapter 8: Putting Together an Assemblage

Putting together an assemblage is like completing a puzzle. An assemblage is when two parcels (or more) of land are combined to be sold as one parcel. Typically, the two parcels, when combined, may bring in a larger price than the properties would if they were sold separately. This is a psychological principal known as *Gestalt*.

Psychologist believe that the perceived value of groupings exists in the mind because of an innate disposition to perceive patterns. The principles that we use to perceive the patterns are organized into five categories: Proximity, Similarity, Continuity, Closure, and Connectedness.

The goal of an assemblage play is to find a group of properties that, when combined, can be made into one parcel that will be worth a great deal more than if you simply added up the value of each individual existing parcel. Pulling off a successful assemblage requires a great deal of imagination, planning and nerve.

One of the great assemblages occurred in Florida in the 1960s, when The Walt Disney Company made a number of purchases to assemble a large piece of land for an amusement complex.

How did Disney go and buy up thousands of acres of land without the landowners holding out for exorbitant prices? Disney set up dozens of "dummy" corporations, with names like "M.T. Lott" (get it? Empty Lot?), the "Latin-American Development and Managers Corporation" and the "Reedy Creek Ranch Corporation" to purchase seemingly worthless parcels of land, ranging from swampland to cattle pastures.

In late June of 1965, the *Orlando Sentinel* reported in an article that over 27,000 acres had recently changed hands. Speculation began that large corporations such as Ford, McDonnell-Douglas, Hughes Aircraft, and Boeing, (as Kennedy Space Center was located nearby), and, yes, even Disney. In October, the *Orlando Sentinel* released the story that it was Disney who had been behind the purchases. Once that was revealed, Walt bought his first acre of land in Florida for *Walt Disney World* for $80.00 and his last for $80,000.00! Mr. Disney quickly scheduled a press conference and confirmed the story. He described the $400 million dollar project that would become *Walt Disney World*.

In exchange for bringing such a boost to the area's economy, the creation of thousands of jobs, and improvements to the environment and infrastructure of central Florida, Disney was given permission to establish its own autonomous government, known as the Reedy Creek Improvement District.

When Disney purchased the 47 square miles that was to become the *Walt Disney World Resort*, it was nothing more than a desolate swampland, scrub forests, and groves. Since much of central Florida is essentially "floating" on a body of water, a daunting challenge presented itself. Disney had to transform this land, while balancing the needs of the environment and ecology of the area. If any part of the water supply was damaged or deleted, it would have caused a massive ecological imbalance to the region.

In 1970, Disney Corp. set aside a 7,500-acre Conservation Area, which would never be built on. This would preserve cypress trees as well as provide land for the area's natural inhabitants. Second, the company developed an engineering marvel by creating a system of more than 55 miles of canals and levees to control water levels. The mechanisms that control the water levels are completely automated, and require no monitoring and little maintenance. Pretty impressive, considering the property is about twice the size of Manhattan!

Over the years, Disney purchased an additional 3,000 acres, bringing the *Walt Disney World Resort*'s total size to over 30,000 acres. "There's enough land here to hold all the ideas and plans we can possibly imagine," a Disney spokesman said.

Methods to Assemble

When you're putting together an assemblage, make absolutely sure that none of the selling entities gets wind of your plan.

For example, let's say you have an idea to put five real estate parcels together so that you will have one big plot of land on which to erect one larger, more profitable structure as opposed to five smaller, less profitable buildings. Imagine your situation, if you convinced four of the buyers to sell to you and then all of a sudden, the last seller who owns the fifth property finds out about your strategy and becomes a holdout! If the fifth landowner knows you will be making a big profit, the owner will demand an exorbitant price—because he knows you will have to pay it to make the assemblage work.

Here are some interesting stories about hold outs that have occurred throughout the world.

The Gate Tower Building, Osaka

In 1983, the Japanese government made plans to expand the Osaka section of the Hanshin Expressway. They needed a parcel of land for an exit ramp, and the owners were not interested in selling. The family that owned the real estate had run a company there and they wanted to build a new, modern office tower. The two parties settled in for negotiations—five years of them. They finally came to an agreement: The government would grant the owners the permits necessary to build their tower—but only if it could run its highway through part of it. Today, the Hanshin Expressway is listed as the "tenant" of the building's fifth, sixth, and seventh floors, and office workers toil in the rest of the heavily soundproofed building.

The Polderhuis, Rotterdam

When developers came to build a shopping mall in northeastern Rotterdam in the 1990s, they decided to protect a historic home there. The brick manse had been built in 1930, and served as accommodation for those who ran the area's polder, or tract of land reclaimed from the sea. The mall was built so that it contains the Polder House, or Polderhuis, and today the home sits in the middle of an upscale home furnishings store called Rivièra Maison, which displays its wares in the various rooms for customers to peruse. An enormous window allows the house to be seen from the highway that parallels the mall.

Narita Airport Farms, Tokyo

There are farms abutting the runways of Narita Airport. In the 1960s, the Japanese government announced it would buying out around 1,200 farmers. A protest movement was born. The result, according to the *Japan Times*, was "some of the most violent protests in the history of Japanese activism." Six people died in the clashes and the opening of the airport was delayed. When it finally did open, in 1978, only one of the five planned runways was operative. Today, Narita has two runways, and officials are making noises about a third—which means about 200 properties in the surrounding area will need to go, including some farms. Negotiations on compensation for farmers "might take a long time."

Macy's, New York City

Macy's, the ginormous department store that has taken up an entire city block in Manhattan's "Midtown South" since 1902, does not form a complete rectangle. Instead, the retail behemoth has a corner notch in which a five-story building sits. The odd setup goes back to a 19th-century competition between Rowland H. Macy and a rival, Henry Siegel, a partner in Siegel-Cooper, a bygone store. In the 1890s, Rowland Macy began to acquire the land his store now occupies, but before he could purchase the small corner lot at 34th and Broadway, Siegel bought it. Though Macy's has never owned the holdout, it has advertised on its exterior since the 1940s. A billboard made to look like a huge Macy's shopping bag is currently wrapped around the narrow structure, declaring Macy's "the world's largest store."

Spiegelhalter's Jewelry and Clock Store, London

In the 1920s, the small family-owned shop Spiegelhalter's Jewelry and Clock Store, in operation since the early 19th century, refused to sell to Wickham's Department Store. Wickham's Department Store had expanded so much that it owned all the buildings surrounding Spiegelhalter's. Wickham wanted to expand even more by creating a grand building encompassing the entire block. The Spiegelhalter's jewelry store owners wouldn't budge. Wickham built around it. It is an off-kilter building, with a tower that was supposed to rise from its center positioned off to one side. Over a century later and decades since either store has been in operation, developers were planning a new office complex. It became clear that their plans included demolishing Spiegelhalter's and replacing it with a tall, glass atrium, local groups campaigned to save it. The developers said they will keep Spiegelhalter's facade intact—making it a two-time holdout.

Coking House, Atlantic City, N.J.

In 1961, Vera Coking and her husband bought the property at 127 South Columbia Place for $20,000.

In the 1970s, she was offered $1 million for her property in order to build a Hotel and Casino. She declined the offer. In 1978, construction was started around the Coking house, but ran out of money in 1980. Construction stopped. The steel framework structure was finally torn down in 1993.

In 1993, the owner of a nearby Atlantic City casino and hotel, bought several surrounding lots intending to build a parking lot. Coking refused to sell, again. As a result, the city condemned her house, using the power of eminent domain. She was offered

$251,000, a quarter of what she was offered 10 years earlier.

With the assistance of the Institute for Justice, Coking fought the local authorities and eventually prevailed. Property records show that in 2010, Coking transferred ownership of the house to her daughter, who put it on the market in 2011. The property was finally sold for $583,000 in an auction on July 31, 2014.

Here are some defensive and offensive tactics you can apply when putting together an assemblage.

Using Straw Buyers

Technically, a straw buyer is someone who buys something on behalf of someone else. If you want to buy five parcels of land without making people become suspicious, you can arrange for five people or five LLCs (Limited Liability Companies) to buy the properties.

Presently, it is hard for someone to find out who is exactly inside an LLC. Therefore, you could own all of the LLCs that buy each parcel of land. Then, once you have acquired all of them, you can sell or transfer all five of them into another entity that you would control.

The straw buyers would have to be people you can trust; who can go along with your plan, and carry it out well without any mistakes. One challenge is that the sellers will ask these LLCs for their financial history, and they will want to check out the creditworthiness of these LLCs. Of course, they will not have any financial or credit history. Since it will be difficult to secure loans, you will be boxed into a situation where you will have to put a great deal of money down on each parcel.

Calculated Patience

Another strategy to be a good assembler is to simply have a great deal of patience. You can purchase one or two parcels of property adjacent or near to one another at first. Then, over time, as properties next to or near you become available, you buy them. This could take quite a long time. But some of the most famous assemblage experts in New York City have waited for a decade or more to make the right, perfect assemblage.

Adding Air Rights

Aside from assembling the physical parcels of land or properties you can also tie in the air rights to an assemblage. Perhaps one or two parcel owners already sold their air rights or have built their structure to the highest allowable Floor Area Ratio (FAR). Floor area ratio (FAR) is the ratio of a building's total floor area (gross floor area) to the size of the piece of land upon which it is built. The term can also refer to limits imposed on such a ratio through zoning. In essence, you combine all of the actual parcels and all of the air rights to make a design that maximizes the joining of all these elements.

Chapter 9: Bifurcating a Business

The word "bifurcate" comes from Latin, and refers to dividing something into two parts, like the business end of a fork. One of the most creative plays in commercial real estate investing is the strategy of buying a concern, then turning around and selling it to one party—and then selling the property it inhabits to another party. In some case, you can sell off other components of the business aside from the core business and the real property.

The goal is to buy the entire enterprise for a low price and then sell the components so that the income you generate from the sale of the components is much greater than what you paid for the whole.

Let's look at some examples. Please note that the following are merely examples to illustrate the concept. The numbers are made up, but are reasonable. The lesson here is to understand the concept.

Imagine an engineering company called *The American Engineers Corporation*. They perform engineering services such as engineering plans for office buildings, site surveys of land, and load calculations for bridges. The company's owner has decided to retire and sell the business.

The business may be doing okay because the company does not have the best technology but has a good core of loyal clients—even though the client base has dwindled over the years. The company is making a small profit. It has a main building, a garage for its small fleet of field vehicles, an excellent reputation, and popular name—plus a 40-year history. You buy this "almost break even" business for $300,000.

The core engineering business is transferable, so you can sell the business to another engineering company. In regard to the employees, I would recommend that you do the ethical thing and try to negotiate a deal by which all or most of the employees can be transferred over to the new company with the same compensation or maybe even more.

Then you sell off the components as follows:
- The business is sold for $150,000.
- The property, which now can be delivered vacant to an investor, is sold for $225,000.
- The brand name can be sold to a new, young company that wants to give the impression that they have been around for a long time. The price for the brand name could be $40,000. For example, perhaps the young company that buys just the brand name is called The Smith Engineering Firm.

They can now buy the brand name and rebrand their company logo to (say):

The Smith Engineering Company—A Division of The American Engineers Corporation Since 1980

The fleet vehicles may also be sold if the new purchasing company does not need them or want them. So perhaps the vehicles can generate another $30,000.

Your proceeds, added up:

Business	$150,000
Property	$225,000
Brand Name	$40,000
Vehicles	$30,000
Total	$445,000

Your profit: $145,000. You would make approximately 48% on your investment!

Chapter 10: Land

Investing in land could be a riskier venture than most because it may take a long time for the land to increase in value substantially enough to make a good profit. I suggest you do not buy land right in the center of a hot market, because you will be competing with sophisticated developers who will buy the property to develop a structure on it. That is where they will make their big money: selling the final constructed building, or selling the condos or co-ops, or renting the apartments, stores, or offices. Their big profit is not in how low they can buy the land; rather, it's a matter of timing the market and making the profit on the units they will be selling or renting.

To buy low and sell high you need to first find a piece of land that is in a "path of development." Markets do not only move up and down; they also have direction. If you look at a locale over a period of time—say, five to 10 years—you can see a path of new development, or a path of gentrification. So, the way to get the best value for your money is to buy a property that is near that path of development—not too close or you will overpay, and not too far because it may take an eternity for the hot market to reach you.

Of course, the timing on this depends on the buyer. Some people can wait for five years to sell their land

and make a profit. Some have much greater patience and can wait 10 or even 20 years.

Keep in mind that banks do not like to lend money to an investor to buy land. So, you may need to pay all cash to obtain the deed. Also, you will need to pay the annual real estate taxes—and most likely you will not be getting any income (rent) from the unimproved land. (Unimproved land is defined as land that does not have certain basic required services necessary to put it to other purposes: electricity, telephone, street access, water, etc.

When the market does come to your property, you will have two basic strategic choices:

1. Just Sell

    Simply resell to the highest bidder. This is straightforward. Let's say you bought 10 acres of unimproved land for $100,000 cash and five years later you were able to sell it for $130,000. Your gross profit is $30,000— however you had to pay $1,000 per year on real estate taxes, so your net profit was $25,000. In other words, you made $5,000 for each year you held onto the land, which is a five percent profit on your money.

2. Throw the land into a deal

You can take your land and "contribute" it into a deal with a developer. Why would you give a developer your completely-paid-off land? To make a lot more money than if you had just sold it. Why would a developer want to partner up with you and accept your land as part of the deal? It will make it a lot easier for him to get a construction loan from the bank.

There are many variations to this type of deal but here are the core deal components:

Developers need to preserve their cash and try to leverage as much as they can. Traditionally, they have to get an Acquisition and Development loan. If you partner up with them, they can go to the bank and show that the entity that is going to own the land and build upon it already has the land. In other words, the entity already has equity in the deal.

Land can sometimes constitute 25 percent of the value of the final product. Of course, this percentage can vary quite a lot due to zoning rules, height restrictions, FAR, setbacks, etc.

So, let's look at our example of 10 acres of land, worth $100,000.

You and the developer form a new entity, preferably an LLC. You negotiate the deal so that the developer owns 80% of the LLC and you own 20%.

You also negotiate these key points:
- You are the "first one out."
- You are not subject to a cash call.

The developer can build eight houses with one-acre lots. (Note; 20% of the land—two acres—will be required for roads, and public areas.) Each house will cost $200,000 to build and will be sold for $350,000. The developer will make $150,000 profit per house or a total of $1,200,000.

Since you own 20 percent of the LLC you will receive $240,000: much more than your property's appraised value of $125,000.

Here are some cautionary tips if you pursue this type of commercial real estate investment:

Zoning

Before you invest in land be sure that the present zoning will allow for the desired project you may want to build on the site—by yourself or with a partner such as a home builder or a developer. If you partner with an experienced, successful builder, he should have a good handle on the probability that the land will be lawfully allowed to accommodate the proposed project.

Deed Restrictions

Sometimes a deed will include some kind of restriction or covenant. These are different from zoning, and usually make the development of the land problematic. It is critical that one of the first things you investigate when you buy land is if there are any deed restrictions on the land. You will find this information by reading the deed.

Zoning is a type of control that is placed on a property by the government, usually the local municipality. The government maintains zoning policies primarily to control density and it is done for the good of all the people in a community. A deed restriction, on the other hand, is a legal right, which a property owner can place on his own property.

Some deed restrictions can be placed on the land in perpetuity. In other words, if there is a deed restriction on the land you bought, and it is stated that the restriction is for perpetuity, it could limit your abilities in regard to building upon the land.

Wetlands

If a property is partially or completely designated a wetland, you may not be able to build on the land. Many people have been taken advantage of because they thought they were buying a very inexpensive, way-below-market piece of land, with the intent of building a beautiful home on it—then learning that the area is a wetland and they would never be allowed to build anything on it.

A wetland is defined as a land area that is either permanently or seasonally saturated with water, typically having characteristics of a distinct ecosystem. Some examples include swamps, marshes, and bogs. These bodies of water can contain either fresh, brackish, or salt water.

Wetland designations are managed by both State and federal regulations. Wetlands are regulated by the U.S. Army Corps of Engineers (Corps) and the U.S. Environmental Protection Agency (EPA) or by the state or local government. In New York the DEC maintains control over the delineation of wetlands and will have a biologist demarcate the wetland lines. In some cases, federal or local government may take over the land to preserve it.

Setbacks

These are another tool that the local government uses to make sure that citizens build structures properly on a site.

"Setbacks are building restrictions imposed on property owners. Local governments create setbacks through ordinances and Building Codes, usually for reasons of public policy such as safety, privacy, and environmental protection. Setbacks prevent landowners from crowding the property of others, allow for the safe placement of pipelines, and help to preserve wetlands. Setbacks form boundaries by establishing an exact distance from a fixed point, such as a property line or an adjacent structure, within which building is prohibited. Generally, prospective buyers learn that land is subject to setback provisions when they are considering purchasing it. This information is important to future development plans, because setbacks remain in effect until changed by law or special action of a local government.

Setbacks can significantly affect a property owner's right to develop land or to modify existing structures on the land. For this reason they can influence property values; severe restrictions on land can decrease its value. Violating setback provisions can lead to legal action against a property owner, and penalties can include fines as well as an order to remove noncompliant structures. Property owners whose desire to build is stymied by setbacks have few remedies. They can petition their local government by applying for a variance—a special permission to depart from the requirements of Zoning ordinances—but variances are generally granted only in cases of extreme hardship. Litigation over setbacks is common." As defined by https://legal-dictionary.thefreedictionary.com/Setbacks.

Setbacks are essential to regulation of real estate for several reasons. They might serve to ensure that an emergency vehicle could drive between two buildings to get to the back of one of them. They might ensure better visual access, ventilation, natural light, insulation from ambient sound, access to services, and better gardens and landscapes between habitable spaces and traffic outside. Setbacks simply help to make a neighborhood look nicer, by ensuring more open spaces, plus semi-covered and covered spaces to give a sense of ease and welcome to a building.

There are front yard, side yard and back yard setbacks. For example, the rule might be that is someone wishes to build a house on a piece of land that the structure must be 80 feet from the neighbor's house on both sides of the proposed house. The building must be set back 100 feet from the front sidewalk, etc.

Another crucial item to investigate is the required footage of all the setbacks. Whatever you intend to build will be impacted by the setbacks. Setbacks can significantly reduce the amount of square footage you can build upon a property.

Chapter 11: TIC Investment

TICs--The acronym TIC stands for Tenants in Common. It refers to the type of ownership in a real estate property. You might think it means a group of apartment tenants living in the same unit, but, no. It is a legal term to describe ownership but it has also been used to describe a type of property.

In a TIC situation, the property is owned by a group of people who may or may not have the same percentage of ownership. Another key point is that if one of the owners dies, his percentage share of the property will go to his heirs. This is important to note because in some other forms of ownership, if one of the owners dies, his share of the property goes to the other owners.

This is an attractive option to some investors, since you do not need a lot of money to invest in a TIC. By buying into a TIC, you maximize your ability to invest. By contributing a small investment to the TIC, you might own a piece of a very large property. Better yet (for some investors), you have no headaches in regard to managing a property. It is a purely passive investment.

One of the most important differences between investing in a TIC, and investing in a REIT, is that when you invest in a REIT you are investing in a group of properties. Investing in a TIC means investing in one property. REITS take your money and buy and sell properties. Quite often you will not know which ones they are going to sell or which ones they are going to buy.

A TIC is created by someone referred to as the sponsor of the investment. A sponsor will carry out the following functions to get the TIC started:

- find the property to buy;
- negotiate the purchase and get the property in the contract;
- perform the due diligence
- obtain the proper financing;
- complete the TIC sales;
- physically manage of the property or hire someone to manage it;
- distribute the monthly disbursements and reports;
- sell the property.

Cautionary Tips

Some TIC sponsors do not have real estate experience. Many of them come from the stock securities industry. Lack of experience can lead to bad decision-making—such as obtaining poor information on pricing, or an inaccurate appraisal.

Conclusion

Chapter 12: Conclusion

The key to becoming a successful commercial real estate investor, and maintaining success, is to gradually diversify your investments into a large and lucrative portfolio. One of the key goals of this book is to give you insight into how to lay out your investment plans.

When the market related to one of the investment categories discussed in this book is in a down cycle, you should try to invest in it. For example, if the economy is down, perhaps you should focus on buying that first three-family house, improve the property over time, and collect a good income.

If at some point in your life you do not have a great deal of extra liquid cash but still want to invest in real estate, consider investing in REITS. Don't just buy one REIT. You should eventually buy a REIT in each of the categories listed in Chapter 7.

You may be blessed with physical youthfulness or may have a youthful spirit or mentality. If so, it may be a good time to invest in commercial real estate that requires stamina to get things done. As you age you may want to add into your portfolio those investments that are not so physically demanding.

Ideally, over the course of your life you should accumulate—or at least consider acquiring—all of the types of investments outlined in this handbook.

I hope my thoughts and recommendations have helped you set out a good plan for your future investments and has given you food for thought on the many assets and strategies that you can pursue.

Please see the following chart on page 124..

Chart Explanation:

The use of the word "High" means you need a lot more of the items relative to the other categories.

For example: High *Capital* in *NNN Tenant* means you need a lot more money to purchase *NNN Tenant* properties than how much money you need to buy some REIT stocks that are shown as Low in the chart.

"Low" means you do not need as much as compared to others.

For example: Low in regard to *Physical Ability* for *Financing* means you will only be required to sign papers and not do heavy labor, whereas High in *Physical Ability* for *Multi-Family* means you may be doing the actual maintenance on the property, mowing lawns, painting, cleaning, etc.

Proximity Yes and No: To give someone *Financing* you do not have to be in physical Proximity and hence the No. However, for *Rezoning*, since there may be many meetings with architects, engineers, builders, planners and zoning boards, it is best to be near the property in question.

Ten Best Ways to Invest in Commercial Real Estate

	Multi-family	Rezoning	NNN Tenant	Retail Condo	REITs	Assemblage	Bifurcating	Land	TICS
Capital	High	High	High	High	Low	High	High	Low	Low
Time	High	High	Low	Low	Low	High	High	Low	Low
Talent	High	High	Low	Low	Low	High	Low	Low	Low
Physical Ability	High	Low	Low	High	Low	Low	Low	Low	Low
Time to Reap	Low	High	Low	Low	Low	High	Low	High	High
Proximity	Yes	Yes	Yes	Yes	No	Yes	No	Yes	No

Notes:

A

abstract of title A summary of all of the recorded instruments and proceedings that affect the title to property, arranged in the order in which they were recorded.

accessory use Land uses within a property that are, in addition to the parcel's principal use, customary, appropriate, subordinate, incidental to, and serve the principal use. The governing body often includes in its zoning ordinance specific accessory uses it believes meet these criteria, but as an example, typical residential accessory uses include garages, decks, swimming pools and storage sheds.

accretion The addition of land through processes of nature, as by water or wind.

accrued interest Accrue; to grow; to be added to. Accrued interest is interest that has been earned but not due and payable.

acknowledgment A formal declaration before a duly authorized officer by a person who has executed an instrument that such execution is the person's act and deed.

acquisition An act or process by which a person procures property.

acre A measure of land equaling 43,560 square feet.

action for specific performance A court action to compel a defaulting principal to comply with the provisions of a contract.

adjacent Lying near, but not necessarily in actual contact with.

adjoining Contiguous; attaching, in actual contact with.

administrator A person appointed by the court to administer the estate of a deceased person who left no will; i.e., who died intestate.

ad valorem According to valuation.

adverse possession A means of acquiring title where an occupant has been in actual, open, notorious, exclusive, and continuous occupancy of property under a claim of right for the required statutory period.

aesthetic regulation These are zoning regulations that maintain aesthetic features within a district by permitting only uses, designs, and structures that conform to or complement the area's existing uses and structures. Examples include limitations on parking, setbacks, the colors and architecture of structures, and types of landscaping, roofs, and building materials.

affidavit A statement or declaration reduced to writing and sworn to or affirmed before some officer authorized to administer an oath or affirmation.

affirm To confirm, to ratify, to verify.

agency That relationship between principal and agent that arises out of a contract either expressed or implied, written or oral, wherein an agent is employed by a person to do certain acts on the person's behalf in dealing with a third party.

agent One who undertakes to transact some business or to manage some affair for another by authority of the latter.

agreement of sale A written agreement between seller and purchaser in which the purchaser agrees to buy certain real estate and the seller agrees to sell upon terms and conditions set forth therein.

air rights Rights in real property to use the space above the surface of the land.

alienation A transferring of property to another; the transfer of property and possession of lands, or other things, from one person to another.

alienation clause Allows a lender to require the balance of a loan to be paid in full if the collateral is sold (also known as a "due on sale" clause).

amortization 1) A gradual paying off of a debt by periodic installments. 2)When a building or use becomes non-conforming due to a change in zoning regulations, the property will be given a period of time to comply with the new regulations. This period of time is called the amortization period. If a property is not compliant within the amortization period, the use will be prohibited.

ancillary uses Such uses are permitted land uses that are secondary and complementary to the principal use, but not accessory. An example of an ancillary use is an office supply store in an office park that only serves the principal office uses within the district.

apportionment Adjustment of the income, expenses, or carrying charges of real estate usually computed to the date of closing of title so that the seller pays all expenses to that date. The buyer assumes all expenses commencing the date the deed is conveyed to the buyer.

appraisal An estimate of a property's value by an appraiser who is usually presumed to be expert in the field.

appraisal by cost approach Adding together all parts of a property separately appraised to form a whole; e.g., the value of the land considered as vacant added to the cost of reproduction of the building, less depreciation.

appraisal by income capitalization approach An estimate of value by capitalization of productivity and income.

appraisal by sale comparison approach Comparability with the sales prices of other similar properties.

appurtenance Something that is outside the property itself but belongs to the land and adds to its greater enjoyment, such as a right-of-way or a barn or a dwelling.

assessed valuation A valuation placed upon property by a public officer or a board, as a basis for taxation.

assessment A charge against real estate made by a unit of government to cover a proportionate cost of an improvement, such as a street or sewer.

assessor An official who has the responsibility of determining assessed values.

assignee The person to whom an agreement or contract is assigned.

assignment The method or manner by which a right or contract is transferred from one person to another.

assignor A party who assigns or transfers an agreement or contract to another.

assumption of mortgage The taking of title to property by a grantee, wherein the grantee assumes liability for payment of an existing note or bond secured by a mortgage against a property and becomes personally liable for the payment of such mortgage debt.

avulsion A sudden and perceptible loss or addition to land by the action of water, or a sudden change in the bed or course of a stream.

B

balloon mortgage payment A large payment during the term of a mortgage, often at the end.

beneficiary The person who receives or is to receive the benefits resulting from certain acts.

bequeath To give or hand down by will; to leave by will.

bequest That which is given by the terms of a will.

bill of sale A written instrument given to pass title of personal property from vendor to vendee.

binder An agreement to cover the down payment for the purchase of real estate as evidence of good faith on the part of the purchaser.

blanket mortgage A mortgage covering more than one property. A blanket mortgage is often used for subdivision financing.

blockbusting The practice of inducing homeowners in a particular neighborhood to sell their homes quickly, often at below market prices, by creating the fear that the entry of a minority group or groups into the neighborhood will cause a precipitous decline in property values.

bona fide In good faith, without fraud.

bond The evidence of a personal debt that is secured by a mortgage or other lien on real estate.

building code Regulations established by state or local governments stating fully the structural requirements for building.

building line A line fixed at a certain distance from the front and/or sides of a lot, beyond which no building can project.

building loan agreement An agreement whereby the lender advances money to an owner primarily in the erection of buildings. Such funds are commonly advanced in installments as the structure is completed.

building permit Written governmental permission for the construction, renovation, or substantial repair of a building.

bulk regulations These regulations control the size and layout of structures, including regulations as to open space, lot lines, maximum building height, and maximum floor area ratio.

buffer zones When two adjacent districts have incompatible permitted uses, in order to reduce the conflict between the uses, the governing body may require a buffer zone. Typically such zones will include park areas, grass, trees or berming. Such zones are commonly used when the development of a multi-family complex is proposed adjacent to a single-family district.

C

cancellation clause A provision in a lease or other contract that confers upon one or more of all of the parties to the lease the right to terminate the party's or parties' obligations thereunder upon the occurrence of the condition or contingency set forth in the said clause.

capital appreciation The appreciation accruing to the benefit of the capital improvement to real estate.

capital asset Any asset of a permanent nature used for the production of income.

capital gain Income that results from the sale of an asset not in the usual course of business. (Capital gains may be taxed at a lower rate than ordinary income.)

capital improvement Any structure erected as a permanent improvement to real estate, usually extending the useful life and value of a property. (The replacement of a roof would be considered a capital improvement.)

capital loss A loss from the sale of an asset not in the usual course of business.

caveat emptor Let the buyer beware. The buyer must examine the goods or property and buy at the buyer's own risk.

cease and desist list Upon the establishment of a cease and desist zone by the Secretary of State, a list of homeowners who have filed owner's statements expressing their wish not to be solicited by real estate brokers or salespersons. Soliciting of listed homeowners by licensees is prohibited. Violators of such prohibition are subject to licensure suspension or revocation.

cease and desist zone A rule adopted by the Secretary of State that prohibits the direct solicitation of homeowners whose names and addresses appear on a cease and desist list maintained by the Secretary. Such rule may be adopted upon the Secretary's determination that some homeowners within a defined geographic area have been subject to intense and repeated solicitation by real estate brokers and salespersons.

certificate of occupancy (CO) A document issued by a governmental authority that a building is ready and fit for occupancy.

chain of title A history of conveyances and encumbrances affecting a title from the time the original patent was granted, or as far back as records are available.

chattel Personal property, such as household goods.

client The one by whom a broker is employed.

closing date The date upon which the property is conveyed by the seller to the buyer.

cloud on the title An outstanding claim or encumbrance that, if valid, would affect or impair the owner's title.

collateral Additional security pledged for the payment of an obligation.

color of title That which appears to be good title, but that is not title in fact.

commercial use These uses, permitted only in commercial districts, typically include wholesale, retail, or service business uses operating for profit, including office uses.

commingling To mingle or mix, for example, a client's funds in the broker's personal or general account.

commission A sum due a real estate broker for services in that capacity.

commitment A pledge or a promise; affirmation agreement.

completion bond A bond used to guarantee that a proposed subdivision development will be completed.

comprehensive/general plan A long-term planning instrument, these plans set forth policies for the future development of the jurisdiction in a manner that will satisfy the jurisdiction's goals, e.g., maintain orderly growth and protect the general welfare. Comprehensive plans often include local area plans, land use-related resolutions by the governing body, maps, and policy statements.

condemnation Taking private property for public use, with fair compensation to the owner; exercising the right of eminent domain.

conditional sales contract A contract for the sale of property stating that delivery is to be made to the buyer, title to remain vested in the seller until the conditions of the contract have been fulfilled.

conditional use These uses are permitted on a permanent basis within a district so long as the governing body's conditions are met. These uses require conditions because without them, they could negatively impact the parcel or bordering properties. Permits for conditional uses are given at the discretion of the governing body.

consideration Anything given to induce another to enter into a contract, such as money or personal services.

constructive notice Information or knowledge of a fact imputed by law to a person because the person could have discovered the fact by proper diligence and inquiry(e.g., via public records).

contingency A provision in a contract that requires the occurrence of a specific event before the contract can be completed.

contract An agreement between competent parties to do or not to do certain things that is legally enforceable, whereby each party acquires a right.

contract zoning Contract zoning occurs when a property owner and the governing body enter an agreement that the property will be rezoned and the owner will accept the body's use and design restrictions.

conversion Change from one character or use to another.

conveyance The transfer of the title of land from one to another; the means or medium by which title of real estate is transferred.

covenants Agreements written into deeds and other instruments promising performance or non-performance of certain acts, or stipulating certain uses or non-uses of the property.

cul-de-sac A blind alley; a street with only one outlet.

cumulative zoning Under this zoning scheme, property zoned for specific uses can be used for that use and for less intensive uses. For example, an area zoned for multi-family uses would also permit a single-family use within the parcel.

current value The value usually sought to be estimated in an appraisal.

D

damages The indemnity recoverable by a person who has sustained an injury, either to his or her person, property, or relative rights, through the act or default of another.

debit The amount charged as due or owed.

density Density is the amount of development allowed per acre, and typically calculated by the number of dwelling units per acre (for residential) or floor area ratio (for commercial).

discriminatory/exclusionary zoning This type of zoning refers to a community's use of zoning regulations to exclude certain groups of people. Though it is unlawful to expressly exclude people based on race or ethnicity, regulations relating to development densities can still have exclusionary effects. For example, communities will limit the number of dwellings permitted, reducing the housing supply, and thus lowering opportunities for new buyers. Further, reducing the housing supply increases market prices, having the effect of excluding lower-income families. Similarly, zoning regulations that limit or prohibit low-income multi-family complexes have the direct effect of excluding lower-income households from residing in the community.

down-zoning Down-zoning occurs when a parcel is rezoned to a classification permitting only less intensive uses. Communities will utilize down-zoning to limit less-desired intensive uses. For example, a community may rezone a parcel from a multi-family designation to a single-family district.

duress Unlawful constraint exercised upon a person whereby the person is forced to do some act against the person's will.

E

earnest money Down payment made by a purchaser of real estate as evidence of good faith.

easement A right that may be exercised by the public or individuals on, over, or through the lands of others.

economic life The period over which a property will yield the investor a return on the investment.

economic obsolescence Lessened desirability or useful life arising from economic forces, such as changes in optimum land use, legislative enactments that restrict or impair property rights, and changes in supply-demand ratios.

ejectment A form of action to regain possession of real property, with damages for the unlawful retention; used when there is no relationship of landlord and tenant.

eminent domain A right of the government to acquire property for necessary public use by condemnation. The owner must be fairly compensated.

encroachment A building, part of a building, or obstruction that intrudes upon or invades a highway or sidewalk or trespasses upon the property of another.

encumbrance Any right to or interest in the land interfering with its use or transfer, or subjecting it to an obligation (Also *incumbrance).*

endorsement An act of signing one's name on the back of a check or note, with or without further qualifications.

equity The interest or value that the owner has in real estate over and above the liens against it.

equity loan Junior loan based on a percentage of the equity.

equity of redemption A right of the owner to reclaim property before it is sold through foreclosure proceedings, by the payment of the debt, interest, and costs.

erosion The wearing away of land through processes of nature, as by water and winds.

escheat The reversion to the State of property in the event the owner thereof abandons it or dies, without leaving a will and has no distributees to whom the property may pass by lawful descent.

escrow A written agreement between two or more parties providing that certain instruments or property be placed with a third party to be delivered to a designated person upon the fulfillment or performance of some act or condition.

estate The degree, quantity, nature, and extent of interest that a person has in real property.

estate at will The occupation of lands and tenements by a tenant for an indefinite period, terminable by one or both parties at will.

estate in reversion The residue of an estate left for the grantor, to commence in possession after the termination of some particular estate granted by the grantor.

estoppel certificate An instrument executed by the mortgagor setting forth the present status and the balance due on the mortgage as of the date of the execution of the certificate.

eviction A legal proceeding by a landlord to recover possession of real property from a tenant.

eviction, actual Where one is, either by force or by process of law, actually put out of possession.

eviction, constructive Any disturbance of the tenant's possession of the leased premises by the landlord whereby the premises are rendered unfit or unsuitable for the purpose for which they were leased.

exclusive agency An agreement of employment of a broker to the exclusion of all other brokers. If sale is made by any other broker during term of employment, broker holding exclusive agency is entitled to commissions in addition to the commissions payable to the broker who effected the transaction.

exclusive right to sell An agreement of employment by a broker under which the exclusive right to sell for a specified period is granted to the broker. If a sale during the term of the agreement is made by the owner or by any other broker, the broker holding such exclusive right to sell is nevertheless entitled to compensation.

executor A male person or a corporate entity or any other type of organization named or designed in a will to carry out its provisions as to the disposition of the estate of a deceased person.

executrix A woman appointed to perform the same duties as an executor.

extension agreement An agreement that extends the life of a mortgage to a later date.

exactions New development will often increase the use of, and the need for, improved or new public infrastructure and facilities, e.g., water and sewer lines, road improvements, and parks. Exactions are how a community forces developers to contribute to the cost of such infrastructure. They can take the form of requiring a developer to pay for a portion of the infrastructure improvements necessitated by the development, impact fees, or the donation of a portion of the developer's land. (Do You Know These Essential Zoning Terms?, 2016)

F

fee; fee simple; fee absolute Absolute ownership of real property; a person has this type of estate where the person is entitled to the entire property with unconditional power of disposition during the person's life and descending to the person's heirs or distributes.

fiduciary A person who, on behalf of or for the benefit of another, transacts business or handles money or property not the person's own; such relationship implies great confidence and trust.

fixtures Personal property so attached to the land or improvements as to become part of the real property.

floor area ratio (FAR) is the ratio of a building's total floor area (gross floor area) to the size of the piece of land upon which it is built. The terms can also refer to limits imposed on such a ratio through zoning. (Floor area ratio, 2019)

floating zones These are districts that are permitted under the zoning ordinance, but not placed on the zoning map. They are typically used for unique uses (e.g., major entertainment centers, intensive industrial uses) that are anticipated in the future, but no specific location has been identified within the community. When an application is made for such a use on a specific parcel, a floating zone can be established and located on the zoning map, provided the regulations set forth in the zoning ordinance are met.

foreclosure A procedure whereby property pledged as security for a debt is sold to pay the debt in the event of default in payments or terms.

freehold An interest in real estate, not less than an estate for life. (Use of this term discontinued September 1, 1967.)

G

grace period Additional time allowed to perform an act or make a payment before a default occurs.

graduated leases A lease that provides for a graduated change at stated intervals in the amount of the rent to be paid; used largely in long-term leases.

grant A technical term used in deeds of conveyance of lands to indicate a transfer.

grandfather clauses The term "grandfathering" is a misnomer for a legal prior non-conforming use. A "grandfathering" situation occurs when an existing use was in compliance with zoning regulations at the time it began, but changes to the regulations have caused the use to become non-conforming. If the owner sells the property, the buyer will have the right to continue the non-conforming use, causing people to label the use as "grandfathered." However, because this situation is simply the transfer of a lawful non-conforming use, the laws related to such uses create certain limitations, e.g., the use may not continue indefinitely as it will be subject to an amortization period, and the use cannot be expanded.

grantee The party to whom the title to real property is conveyed.

grantor The person who conveys real estate by deed; the seller.

gross income Total income from property before any expenses are deducted.

gross lease A lease of property whereby the lessor is to meet all property charges regularly incurred through ownership.

ground rent Earnings of improved property credited to earnings of the ground itself after allowance made for earnings of improvements.

group boycott An agreement between members of a trade to exclude other members from fair participation in the trade.

H

habendum clause The "to have and to hold" clause that defines or limits the quantity of the estate granted in the premises of the deed.

holdover tenant A tenant who remains in possession of leased property after the expiration of the lease term.

I

incompetent A person who is unable to manage his or her own affairs by reason of insanity, imbecility, or feeblemindedness.

industrial uses These uses are non-residential, non-agricultural, and non-commercial uses such as mining, milling, and manufacturing. Zoning ordinances generally include many classes of industrial uses, and the regulation of each varies depending on the intensity and impact of the use. Common examples of light industrial uses are warehouses, manufacturing and distribution where they operate without negative impacts on the surrounding uses. Heavy industrial uses have the potential to create public nuisance conditions (e.g., noise, environmental impacts), and are thus more stringently located and regulated. Examples of heavy industrial uses include quarries, landfills, and asphalt or concrete mixing plants.

in rem A proceeding against the realty directly; as distinguished from a proceeding against a person. (Used in taking land for nonpayment of taxes, etc.)

installments Parts of the same debt, payable at successive periods as agreed; payments made to reduce a mortgage.

instrument A written legal document; created to *effect* the rights of the parties.

interest rate The percentage of a sum of money charged for its use.

intestate A person who dies having made no will, or leaves one that is defective in form, in which case the person's estate descends to the person's distributees in the manner prescribed by law.

involuntary lien A lien imposed against property without consent of the owner, such as taxes, special assessments.

irrevocable Incapable of being recalled or revoked; unchangeable; unalterable.

J

joint tenancy Ownership of realty by two or more persons, each of whom has an undivided interest with the "right of survivorship."

judgment A formal decision issued by a court concerning the respective rights and claims of the parties to an act or suit.

junior mortgage A mortgage second in lien to a previous mortgage.

L

laches Delay or negligence in asserting one's legal rights; landlord One who rents property to another.

lease A contract whereby, for a consideration, usually termed rent, one who is entitled to the possession of real property transfers such rights to another for life, for a term of years, or at will.

leasehold The interest or estate that a lessee of real estate has therein by virtue of the lessee's lease.

lessee A person to whom property is rented under a lease lessor One who rents property to another under a lease.

lien A legal right or claim upon a specific property that attaches to the property until a debt is satisfied.

life estate The conveyance of title to property for the duration of the life of the grantee.

life tenant The holder of a life estate.

lis pendens A legal document, filed in the office of the county clerk, giving notice that an auction or proceeding is pending in the courts affecting the title to the property. (Not applicable in commission disputes.)

listing An employment contract between principal and agent, authorizing the agent to perform services for the principal involving the latter's property.

littoral rights The right of a property owner whose land borders on a body of water, such as a lake, ocean, or sea, to reasonable use and enjoyment of the shore and water the property borders upon.

M

mandatory Requiring strict conformity or obedience.

marketable title A title that a court of equity considers to be so free from defect that it will enforce its acceptance by a purchaser.

market allocation An agreement between members of a trade to refrain from competition in specific market areas.

market price The actual selling price of a property.

market value The most probable price that a property should bring if exposed for sale in the open market for a reasonable period of time, with both the buyer and seller aware of current market conditions, neither being under duress.

master plan The overall plan for a community's development. A master plan must be consistent with the goals and policies described in the comprehensive/general plan and other local plans, e.g., an area plan. Generally master plans include the location of proposed land uses, description of the types of uses, intensities of uses, and building and structure limitations, though they may also include descriptions of desired parking, open space, and layout.

mechanic's lien A lien given by law upon a building or other improvement upon land, and upon the land itself, to secure the price of labor done upon, and materials furnished for, the improvement.

meeting of the minds Whenever all parties to a contract agree to the substance and terms thereof.

metes and bounds A term used in describing the boundary lines of land, seeing forth all the boundary lines together with their terminal points and angles.

minor A person under an age specified by law; usually under 18 years of age.

mixed-use designation This designation allows for the integration of multiple types of uses within a single district. For example, a development that includes multi-family residential, retail and office uses.

monument A fixed object and point established by surveyors to establish land locations.

moratorium When a governing body is considering the amendment of its zoning ordinance or planning documents, it may decide to enact a temporary ban, a "moratorium," on zoning applications for the uses being considered. Though it is generally accepted that a body has the right to use moratoriums in order for to have time to make sound planning decisions, because landowners seeking to develop their properties will be delayed (or, prevented from developing in the event the ultimate change prohibits the use they intended), the moratorium must be reasonable. In determining reasonableness, courts have considered whether the moratorium advances a legitimate governmental interest, is being made in good faith, and doesn't deprive the landowner of all reasonable use for too long.

mortgage An instrument in writing, duly executed and delivered, that creates a lien upon real estate as security for the payment of a specified debt, which is usually in the form of a bond.

mortgage commitment A formal indication by a lending institution that it will grant a mortgage loan on property in a certain specified amount and on certain specified terms.

mortgagee The party who lends money and takes a mortgage to secure the payment thereof.

mortgage reduction certificate An instrument executed by the mortgagee, setting forth the present status and the balance due on the mortgage as of the date of the execution of the instrument.

mortgagor A person who borrows money and gives a mortgage on the person's property as security for the payment of the debt.

multiple listing An arrangement among Real Estate Board of Exchange members, whereby each broker presents the broker's listings to the attention of the other members so that if a sale results, the commission is divided between the broker bringing the listing and the broker making the sale.

N

net listing A price below which an owner will not sell the property, and at which price a broker will not receive a commission; the broker receives the excess over and above the net listing as the broker's commission.

new urbanism A planning and design concept based primarily on two objectives: that neighborhoods should have a sense of community and be environmentally friendly. To affect these goals, new urbanists lobby and work with communities to create or amend planning and zoning laws to allow neighborhoods with multiple uses, require communities to be designed for pedestrian and car traffic, and require environmentally conscious building designs and construction.

NIMBY An acronym for Not In My Backyard, NIMBY refers to groups that oppose a new land use near their residential property. NIMBY efforts are directed at every type of use they deem incompatible with their residential use, including commercial retail or office uses, industrial or more intensive housing uses. The arguments against such uses near residential neighborhoods include that they will increase car and truck traffic, noise and crime, and lower property values. The power of such opposition is largely political, with a group appealing to their elected officials to deny approval of the opposed project.

non-conforming use A non-conforming use is any use, structure or building that doesn't comply with the applicable zoning regulations. Where the use was originally in compliance, but a regulations change made it non-compliant, the use became a lawful prior non-conforming use (LPNCU). As the name suggests, LPNCUs are lawful, and may continue, but they face certain restrictions. Common restrictions are:

1. the use must be made compliant within a certain period of time (an amortization period),

2. the use cannot be expanded,

3. if the LPNCU is changed, it may not return to the prior use, and

4. where the property is damaged beyond a certain point, it may not be repaired.

non-solicitation order A rule adopted by the Secretary of State that prohibits any or all types of solicitation directed toward homeowners within a defined geographic area. Such rule may be adopted after a public hearing and upon the Secretary's determination that homeowners within the subject area have been subject to intense and repeated solicitations by real estate brokers or salespersons and that such solicitations have caused owners to reasonably believe that property values may decrease because persons of different race, ethnic, religious, or social backgrounds are moving or about to move into such area.

notary public A public officer who is authorized to take acknowledgments to certain classes of documents, such as deeds, contracts, and mortgages, and before whom affidavits may be sworn.

O

Oblige The person in whose favor an obligation is entered into obligor. The person who binds himself or herself to another; one who has engaged to perform some obligation; one who makes a bond.

obsolescence Loss in value due to reduced desirability and usefulness of a structure because its design and construction become obsolete; loss because of becoming old fashioned, and not in keeping with modern means, with consequent loss of income.

open listing A listing given to any number of brokers without liability to compensate any except the one who first secures a buyer ready, willing, and able to meet the terms of the listing, or secures the acceptance by the seller of a satisfactory offer; the sale of the property automatically terminates the listing

open space Open spaces are utilized in zoning ordinances to allow for public or private uses for enjoyment, such as park areas or simply green space. Open space requirements are often calculated as a certain percentage of a parcel's size.

option A right given for a consideration to purchase or lease a property upon specified terms within a specified time. If the right is not exercised the option holder is not subject to liability for damages; if exercised, the grantor of option must perform.

P

partition The division that is made of real property between those who own it in undivided shares.

party wall A wall built along the line separating two properties, partly on each, which either owner, the owner's heirs, and assigns have the right to use; such right constituting an easement over so much of the adjoining owner's land as is covered by the wall.

percentage lease A lease of property in which the rental is based upon the percentage of the volume of sales made upon the leased premises; usually provides for minimum rental.

performance bond A bond used to guarantee the specific completion of an endeavor in accordance with a contract.

personal property Any property that is not real property.

planned unit development (PUD) A mixed-use development (often residential, retail and office) with a cohesive design plan. To encourage the feasibility of such developments, zoning regulations, otherwise required of the individual uses, may be waived or modified to allow for flexibility in the development's design.

plat book A public record containing maps of land showing the division of such land into streets, blocks, and lots, and indicating the measurements of the individual parcels.

plottage Increment in unity value of a plot of land created by assembling smaller ownerships into one ownership.

points Discount charges imposed by lenders to raise the yields on their loans.

police power The right of any political body to enact laws and enforce them, for the order, safety, health, morals, and general welfare of the public.

power of attorney A written instrument duly signed and executed by a person that authorizes an agent to act on his or her behalf to the extent indicated in the instrument.

prepayment clause A clause in a mortgage that gives a mortgagor the privilege of paying the mortgage indebtedness before it becomes due.

price fixing Conspiring to establish fixed fees or prices for services or products.

primary use A primary use is the principal or dominant use of the land, such as residing in a home, running business or manufacturing a product.

principal The employer of an agent or broker; the broker's or agent's client.

probate To establish the will of a deceased person.

purchase money mortgage A mortgage given by a grantee in part payment of the purchase price of real estate.

Q

quiet enjoyment The right of an owner or a person legally in possession to the use of property without interference of possession.

quiet title suit A suit in court to remove a defect, cloud, or suspicion regarding legal rights of an owner to a certain parcel of real property.

quit claim deed A deed that conveys simply the grantor's rights or interest in real estate, without any agreement or covenant as to the nature or extent of that interest, or any other covenants; usually used to remove a cloud from the title.

racial steering The unlawful practice of influencing a person's housing choice based on race.

real estate board An organization whose members consist primarily of real estate brokers and salespersons.

real estate syndicate A partnership formed for participation in a real estate venture; partners may be limited or unlimited in their liability.

realization of gain The taking of the gain or profit from the sale of property.

real property Land, and generally whatever is erected upon or affixed thereto.

Realtor A coined word that may only be used by an active member of a local real estate board, affiliated with the National Association of Real Estate Boards.

reconciliation The final stage in the appraisal process when the appraiser reviews the data and estimates the subject property's value.

recording The act of writing or entering in a book of public record affecting the title to real property.

recourse The right to a claim against a prior owner of a property or note.

redemption The right of a mortgagor to redeem the property by paying a debt after the expiration date and before sale at foreclosure; the right of an owner to reclaim the owner's property after the sale for taxes.

redlining The refusal to lend money within a specific area for various reasons. This practice is illegal.

referee's deed Used to convey real property sold pursuant to a judicial order, in an action for the foreclosure of a mortgage or for partition.

regulatory taking A taking in the real property arena refers to the government exercising its power of eminent domain to acquire ownership of private property for a public use or benefit. A taking is lawful, but the government must pay for the land acquired. A regulatory taking occurs where a governing body enacts regulations that effectively deprive a landowner of all economically reasonable use or value of their property. While the government doesn't actually take title to the property, because the regulations have made the property essentially worthless, it is viewed as a taking, and thus requires compensation to the landowner.

release The act or writing by which some claim or interest is surrendered to another.

release clause A clause found in a blanket mortgage that gives the owner of the property the privilege of paying off a portion of the mortgage indebtedness, and thus freeing a portion of the property from the mortgage.

rem (See *in rem.*)

remainder An estate that takes effect after the termination of a prior estate, such as a life estate.

remainderman The person who is to receive the property after the termination of the prior estate.

rent Compensation paid for the use of real estate.

reproduction cost Normal cost of exact duplication of a property as of a certain date.

residential districts These districts permit residential uses, and typically vary depending on lot size and the number of families that the dwellings in the district are meant to house (e.g., single-family, two-family, etc.). Residential districts for multi-family apartments typically consider the number of units within a defined space (e.g., up to 50 units per acre).

restraint of trade Business practices designed to restrict competition, create a monopoly, control prices, and otherwise obstruct the free operation of business.

restriction A limitation placed upon the use of property contained in the deed or other written instrument in the chain of title.

reversionary interest The interest that a grantor has in lands or other property upon the termination of the preceding estate.

revocation An act of recalling a power of authority conferred, as the revocation of a power of attorney; a license, an agency, etc.

rezoning Change in the zoning district applied to a parcel of land, and thus a change to the permitted uses and accompanying regulations within that parcel.

right of survivorship Right of the surviving joint owner to succeed to the interests of the deceased joint owner; distinguishing feature of a joint tenancy or tenancy by the entirety.

right-of-way The right to pass over another's land pursuant to an easement or license.

riparian owner One who owns land bounding upon a river or water-course.

riparian rights The right of a property owner whose land borders a natural watercourse, such as a river, to reasonable use and enjoyment of the water that flows past the property. Riparian literally means "riverbank."

S

sales contract A contract by which the buyer and seller agree to terms of sale.

satisfaction piece An instrument for recording and acknowledging payment of an indebtedness secured by a mortgage.

second mortgage A mortgage made by a home-buyer in addition to an existing first mortgage.

seizin The possession of land by one who claims to own at least an estate for life therein.

setback The distance from the curb or other established line, within which no buildings may be erected and vary depending on the zoning district.

situs The location of a property.

smart growth Similar to New Urbanism: an urban development and planning concept stressing mixed-used neighborhoods, walkability, and environmentally conscious development and design.

special assessment An assessment made against a property to pay for a public improvement by which the assessed property is supposed to be especially benefited.

specific performance A remedy in a court of equity compelling a defendant to carry out the terms of an agreement or contract.

spot zoning Spot zoning is unlawful, and occurs when a single parcel is zoned differently from surrounding uses for the sole benefit of the landowner. While property may lawfully be zoned differently than surrounding uses, in those cases the uses are typically permitted because they serve a public benefit or a useful purpose to the surrounding properties. For example, sound planning policies would permit a school to be located in the center of a residential neighborhood, but not an adult entertainment store.

Standard State Zoning Enabling Act (SZEA). Federally developed in 1921, SZEA was a standard act on which states could model their own zoning enabling acts. SZEA provided that legislative bodies could divide their jurisdictions into different districts, made a statement of purpose for zoning regulations, and created procedures for establishing such regulations.

statute A law established by an act of the legislature.

statute of frauds State law that provides that certain contracts must be in writing to be enforceable at law.

statute of limitations A statute barring all right of action after a certain period from the time when a cause of action first arises.

subagent An agent of a person already acting as an agent of a principal.

subdivision A tract of land divided into lots or plots.

subletting A leasing by a tenant to another, who holds under the tenant.

subordination clause A clause that permits the placing of a mortgage at a later date that takes priority over an existing mortgage.

subscribing witness One who writes his or her name as witness to the execution of an instrument.

surety One who guarantees the performance of another; guarantor.

surrender The cancellation of a lease by mutual consent of the lessor and the lessee.

surrogate's court (probate court) A court having jurisdiction over the proof of wills, the settling of estates, and of citations.

survey The process by which a parcel of land is measured and its area ascertained; also the blueprint showing the measurements, boundaries, and area.

T

tax sale Sale of property after a period of nonpayment of taxes tenancy at will a license to use or occupy lands and tenements at the will of the owner.

tenancy by the entirety An estate that exists only between husband and wife with equal right of possession and enjoyment during their joint lives and with the "right of survivorship."

tenant One who is given possession of real estate for a fixed period or at-will tenant at sufferance. One who comes into possession of land by lawful title and keeps it afterwards without any title at all.

testate The condition of having a valid will.

tie-in arrangement A contract where one transaction depends upon another.

title Evidence that owner of land is in lawful possession thereof; evidence of ownership.

title insurance A policy of insurance that indemnifies the holder for any loss sustained by reason of defects in the title.

title search An examination of the public records to determine the ownership and encumbrances affecting real property.

Torrens title System of title records provided by state law; a system for the registration of land titles whereby the state of the title, showing ownership and encumbrances, can be readily ascertained from an inspection of the "register of titles" without the necessity of a search of the public records.

Tort A wrongful act, wrong, injury; violation of a legal right.

transfer tax A tax charged under certain conditions on the property belonging to an estate.

U

urban property City property; closely settled property.

usury On a loan, claiming a rate of interest greater than that permitted by law.

V

Valid Having force, or binding force; legally sufficient and authorized.

Valuation Estimated worth or price; the act of valuing by appraisal.

Variance A discretionary, limited waiver or modification of a zoning requirement. It is applied in situations where the strict application of the requirement would result in a practical difficulty or unnecessary hardship for the landowner. Typically, the difficulty or hardship must be due to an unusual physical characteristic of the parcel.

vendee's lien A lien against property under contract of sale to secure deposit paid by a purchaser.

vested rights The vested rights doctrine permits a landowner to build pursuant to a prior zoning regulation when there has been a substantial change of position or expenditures by an innocent party in reliance upon the issuance, or probable issuance, of a building permit. However, where no permit had been issued, and the owner has only an anticipation that it could develop their land under the existing zoning, then a change in zoning prohibiting their anticipated development doesn't create a vested right. Put simply, there is no guarantee that zoning classifications or regulations will stay the same.

violations Act, deed, or conditions contrary to law or permissible use of real property void to have no force or effect; that which is unenforceable.

voidable That which is capable of being adjudged void, but is not, unless action is taken to make it so.

W

Waiver The renunciation, abandonment, or surrender of some claim, right, or privilege.

warranty deed A conveyance of land in which the grantor warrants the title to the grantee

water rights The right of a property owner to use water on, under, or adjacent to the land for such purposes as irrigation, power, or private consumption.

will The disposition of one's property to take effect after death.

wraparound loan A new loan encompassing any zoning ordinance Created in compliance with a governing body's comprehensive plan, zoning ordinances are comprised of maps showing the zoning districts and text setting forth the regulation of uses and structures within each type of district. (Do You Know These Essential Zoning Terms?, 2016)

Index

References

ADA Access to Buildings and Businesses (Public Accommodations) - Overview. (2019). Retrieved from https://civilrights.findlaw.com: https://civilrights.findlaw.com/discrimination/ada-access-to-buildings-and-businesses-public-accommodations.html

Batis, T. C. (n.d.). *Assemblage in Real Estate: Definition & Appraisal.* Retrieved from Study.com: https://study.com/academy/lesson/assemblage-in-real-estate-definition-appraisal.html

Benefits of diversification. (n.d.). Retrieved from ttps://www.dixon.com.au: https://www.dixon.com.au/investment-advice/benefits-of-diversification

COMMUNITY ASSOCIATIONS IN THE UNITED STATES. (n.d.). Retrieved from Community Association Institute: https://www.caionline.org/AboutCommunityAssociations/Pages/StatisticalInformation.aspx

Condominium. (2019, August 22). Retrieved from Wikipedia:

https://en.wikipedia.org/wiki/Condominiu
m

Do You Know These Essential Zoning Terms? (2016, 29
12). Retrieved from
https://propertymetrics.com:
https://propertymetrics.com/blog/do-
you-know-these-essential-zoning-
terms/

Due diligence. (n.d.). Retrieved from
Grammerist.com:
https://grammarist.com/phrase/due-
diligence/

Floor area ratio. (2019, May 22). Retrieved from
Wikipedia.org:
https://en.wikipedia.org/wiki/Floor_area_
ratio

General Post Office, Washington, DC. (n.d.). Retrieved
from https://www.gsa.gov:
https://www.gsa.gov/historic-
buildings/general-post-office-
washington-dc

Haughey, J. (2014, June 26). *Two 'Formula
businesses' OK'd.* Retrieved from
http://www.warwickadvertiser.com:
http://www.warwickadvertiser.com/news/l
ocal-news/two-formula-businesses-okd-
NSWA20140626140629979

Kestenbaum, R. (2018, June 24). *How Retail Real
Estate Continues To Change.* Retrieved from

https://www.forbes.com:
https://www.forbes.com/sites/richardkeste
nbaum/2018/06/24/how-retail-real-
estate-continues-to-
change/#3085c24d7ae1

Kimmons, J. (2018, 11 19). *The Balance-Small Business*. Retrieved from Unimproved Land in Real Estate: https://www.thebalancesmb.com/unimpro ved-land-2867360

Kirk, M. (2017, April 17). *The World's Most Stubborn Real Estate Holdouts*. Retrieved from Citylab.com: https://www.citylab.com/equity/2017/04/t he-worlds-most-stubborn-real-estate-holdouts/523215/

Landsburg, S. F. (2001, March 13). *Putting All Your Potatoes in One Basket*. Retrieved from Slate.com: https://slate.com/culture/2001/03/putting -all-your-potatoes-in-one-basket.html

Mazzara, B. (2016, March 7). *Everything You Need To Know About NYC's Retail Condo Craze*. Retrieved from Biznow: https://www.bisnow.com/new-york/news/retail/everything-you-need-to-know-about-nycs-retail-condo-craze-56759

Mongello, L. (2005, February 11). *Walt Disney World History 101 – "How to buy 27,000 acres of land and have no one notice"*. Retrieved from http://www.wdwradio.com: http://www.wdwradio.com/2005/02/wdw-history-101-how-to-buy-27000-acres-of-land-and-no-one-noticeq/

Mortgage Loan. (2019, Septmber 11). Retrieved from Wikipedia.org: https://en.wikipedia.org/wiki/Mortgage_loan

Obringer, L. A. (2019). *How Mortgages Work.* Retrieved from https://home.howstuffworks.com: https://home.howstuffworks.com/real-estate/buying-home/mortgage2.htm

Orbringer, L. A. (2019). *How REITs Work.* Retrieved from https://home.howstuffworks.com: https://home.howstuffworks.com/real-estate/buying-home/reit.htm

Primary Types of Single-Tenant Net-Leased Properties. (n.d.). Retrieved from JRW Investments: https://www.jrwinvestments.com/articles/asset-classes/primary-types-of-single-tenant-net-leased-properties/

Request for Proposal. (2019, March 27). Retrieved from Wikipedia.org: https://en.wikipedia.org/wiki/Request_for_proposal

Schires, M. (2017, June 6). *A Simple Guide to Using the ADA Standards for Accessible Design Guidelines.* Retrieved from https://www.archdaily.com/: https://www.archdaily.com/872710/a-simple-guide-to-using-the-ada-standards-for-accessible-design-guidelines

SERIES, J. A. (2011). *Legal Aspects of Municipal Historic Preservation.* ALBANY: New York State.

Setback. (n.d.). Retrieved from The Free Dictionary.com: https://legal-dictionary.thefreedictionary.com/Setbacks

Sibley's, Lindsay and Curr Building. (2019, May 24). Retrieved from Wikipedia.org: https://en.wikipedia.org/wiki/Sibley%27s,_Lindsay_and_Curr_Building

Spellen, S. (2012, July 16). *Building of the Day: 420 12th Street.* Retrieved from brownstoner.com: https://www.brownstoner.com/architecture/building-of-the-day-420-12th-street/

State Environmental Quality Review Act. (2019, January 29). Retrieved from Wikipedia.org: https://en.wikipedia.org/wiki/State_Environmental_Quality_Review_Act

Step5: Uniform Land Use Review Procedure (ULURP). (n.d.). Retrieved from

https://www1.nyc.gov:
https://www1.nyc.gov/site/planning/applic
ants/applicant-portal/step5-ulurp-
process.page

The 5 P's of Marketing and Real Estate. (2017,
February 13). Retrieved from
https://www.gateway2realestate.com:
https://www.gateway2realestate.com/post
s/the-5-p-s-of-marketing-and-real-
estate

Vera Coking. (2019, August 29). Retrieved from
Wikipedia.com:
https://en.wikipedia.org/wiki/Vera_Cokin
g

Why diversity is good for investments. (2016, October
16). Retrieved from
https://economictimes.indiatimes.com:
https://economictimes.indiatimes.com/we
alth/plan/why-diversity-is-good-for-
investments/articleshow/54748884.cms?fr
om=mdr

About the Author

Renowned as a foremost negotiations expert, George F. Donohue has been involved

with more real estate negotiations than most real estate professionals in the world today.

He has managed one of the largest real estate portfolios in the world, which included being head of real estate for the World Trade Center in New York City.

Today, he is a corporate executive, author, speaker, consultant, professor, and TV and radio spokesperson.

Mr. Donohue has earned an associate's degree in construction management, a bachelor's degree in architecture, and a Master's Degree in Real Estate Development and Finance at New York University.

Over his lifetime, Mr. Donohue has taught the business of real estate and the art of negotiation to thousands of people. He consults with corporations, governments, and individuals worldwide, and is sought out by the media for his knowledge of real estate, architecture, and business.

Mr. Donohue is a well-known speaker-particularly in China, Japan, and Europe. His assignments have taken him to more than 40 countries around the globe. During his career, he has negotiated with top executives and individuals from entities such as the Japanese, Russian, and French governments, Merrill Lynch, Bank of America, Dean Witter, The Commodities Exchange, the Society of Security Analysts, The Gap, JPMorgan Chase, Citibank, HSBC, Marsh and McLennan, Daiichi Kangyo Bank, Allstate Insurance, Bank of Tokyo, Bank of Taiwan, Duane Reade, McDonald's, Charles Schwab, and hundreds of others.